Dr. Earl Mindell's
AMAZING
APPLE CIDER
VINEGAR

EARL MINDELL, R.PH., PH.D.

Contemporary Books

Chicago New York San Francisco Lisbon London Madrid Mexico City
Milan New Delhi San Juan Seoul Singapore Sydney Toronto

Library of Congress Cataloging-in-Publication Data

Mindell, Earl.
      Dr. Earl Mindell's amazing apple cider vinegar / by Earl Mindell.
          p.   cm.
      Includes bibliographical references and index.
      ISBN 0-658-01461-7 (alk. paper)
        1. Cider vinegar—Health aspects.   2. Cider vinegar—Therapeutic
use.   I. Title: Doctor Earl Mindell's amazing apple cider vinegar.
II. Title: Amazing apple cider vinegar.   III. Title.

RM666.V55 M54   2002
615'.321—dc21   2002023393

Contemporary Books

A Division of The **McGraw·Hill** *Companies*

1 2 3 4 5 6 7 8 9 0   AGM/AGM   1 0 9 8 7 6 5 4 3 2

ISBN 0-658-01461-7

McGraw-Hill books are available at special quantity discounts to use as premiums and sales promotions, or for use in corporate training programs. For more information, please write to the Director of Special Sales, Professional Publishing, McGraw-Hill, Two Penn Plaza, New York, NY 10121-2298. Or contact your local bookstore.

This book is printed on acid-free paper.

CONTENTS

INTRODUCTION

The Miraculous Virtues of Vinegar

You may already use vinegar to dress your salad, wash your windows, or clean out your coffeepot, but you're about to discover a great many more uses for those bottles of pungent liquid that sit on your pantry shelf.

In the pages of this book, you'll find out about vinegar's 10,000-year history as both food and medicine. You'll learn about the different varieties of vinegar made from grains and fruit by cultures around the globe, and about the tastes, healing properties, and brewing methods of vinegars worldwide. If you're a do-it-yourselfer, you'll be pleased to know that I've even included detailed instructions for brewing your own apple cider vinegar. Brewing your own can be challenging, but it's the very best way to be sure your vinegar is chock-full of nutrients and healing power.

Vinegar—especially apple cider vinegar—has some astounding health-protective properties, whether you swallow it or use it topically. I'll tell you about vinegar's uses as a time-honored, trusted home remedy for every ill from acne to yeast infections. Each splash of apple cider vinegar delivers key vitamins, including the antioxidant beta-carotene. It's also bursting with healthful acids, enzymes, a valuable form of dietary fiber called *pectin,* and over a dozen minerals.

Did you know that vinegar is also a useful cosmetic aid? Once you've learned about all the ways vinegar can beautify your skin and hair, you may want to clear a lot of those bottles, jars, and tubes of expensive chemical-laden beauty products out of your life, and replace them with a bottle of the golden elixir made from nature's bountiful apple trees. You can use it to treat unsightly blemishes and itchy insect bites, and it will even help to beautify and freshen your pets!

Homemade vinegar preparations have more household uses than any toxic store-bought chemical. Vinegar is a highly effective and completely nontoxic cleanser, disinfectant, odor eliminator, stain remover, and fabric softener. I'll give you specific recipes for all of these uses and more.

You can use vinegar in every course of a meal, from appetizer to dessert. I'll share with you a few of my favorite recipes that include vinegar, as well as directions for bottling your own delectable and beautiful herb and floral vinegars. Holiday gift giving will be a little easier—just follow the instructions for making these vinegars, tie a ribbon around the neck of the bottle, and presto! You'll be pleasing the eyes and palates of the recipients, as well as supporting their good health.

Once you've read this book, you'll feel good about adding vinegar to your life no matter how or when you do so. As miraculous as these healing and household benefits may be, however, keep in mind that vinegar is only one part of a healthy lifestyle. At the end of this book I'll share with you, in a condensed form, my tips for embracing that beneficial way of living.

Yours in good health,
Dr. Earl Mindell

Chapter One

THE HISTORY AND MAKING OF VINEGAR

It Didn't Just Fall Off the Applecart

As far back as 5000 B.C.E., vinegar was made by the Babylonians, who did this by fermenting the fruit of the date palm. Ancient Egyptian urns dating back to 3000 B.C.E., when analyzed by modern scientists, have been found to contain vinegar residues; early Greek and Roman artwork featured vessels of vinegar. In 400 B.C.E., Hippocrates, the father of modern medicine, prescribed vinegar for a variety of ills.

During Biblical times, vinegar was used to dress wounds and sores, speeding their healing. Vinegar is mentioned no less than eight times in the Bible, with four references in the Old Testament and four in the New Testament. During the time of Jesus Christ, vinegar was valued both as a condiment and a medicine. Ruth 2:14 states, "Boaz said unto her, 'At mealtime comest thou hither, and eat of the bread, and dip the morsel in the vinegar.'" In the Holy Land, two stone jugs were kept in the jails next to the wall where prisoners were bound for flogging. One contained soothing, healing oil, and the other contained antiseptic vinegar.

Warriors through the ages have used vinegar as a strengthening and energizing tonic, as well as for its antiseptic benefits. It is said that during the Great Plague in Europe, enterprising thieves who wished to rob plague victims' houses protected themselves with vinegar against lingering germs. Julius Caesar's armies drank down a vinegar-and-water solution, while Japanese samurai believed that a beverage containing vinegar would boost their strength and help them fight their foes. Records of Hannibal's march over the Alps reveal that when vinegar was poured over hot boulders, they crumbled to make way for troops and elephants to march through. During the Civil War and World War I, vinegar was used to disinfect soldiers' wounds.

Legend has it that Cleopatra dissolved pearls in vinegar and drank the resulting elixir. Christopher Columbus's men counted vinegar among their generous rations aboard those first Spanish ships bound for America. Later, the disease scurvy—caused by lack of vitamin C—was thought to result from the need for acids found in citrus fruits. This belief led to the practice of giving English sailors rations of vinegar to ward off the disease. Soldiers fighting in the American Civil War also sipped vinegar in an attempt to reverse the effects of vitamin C deficiency.

WHAT IS VINEGAR?

Vinegar is what you get when you ferment fruit, grains, or other plants into alcoholic beverages, and then put the resulting liquid through a second fermentation. The first fermentation is carried out by the action of yeasts and is best conducted in a vessel sealed tightly against exposure to oxygen; the second fermentation results from the workings of bacteria and actually requires the presence of oxygen. Apple cider vinegar, for example, is made from two fermentations of the sweet, fresh juice of crushed apples. Grapes are made into wine and then into wine vinegar. Hops and barley are made into beer and then into malt vinegar. Rice is made into rice wine (sake) and then into rice vinegar.

The name *vinegar* comes from the Latin *vinum*, for wine, and *acer*, for sourness or sharpness. *Vinum* plus *acer* became *vinegre*, which in the Latin-rooted French language translates to "sour wine." Over centuries, *vinegre* became the vinegar we know today. In antiquity, vinegar made from beer or ale was known as "ale-gar."

THE ORIGINS OF VINEGAR

Have you ever poured a glass of wine, taken a sip, and found yourself imbibing something much more sour and pungent than the mellow vintage you'd hoped for? The ease with which wine turns to vinegar is a good indication that the discovery of this tart elixir was an accidental by-product of alcoholic beverage production. A bottle of wine left too long can spontaneously turn to vinegar. One day long ago, a jug of wine or beer left uncovered turned sour, and a culinary legend was born. Interestingly, the making of vinegar was not a practice passed from culture to culture; it was discovered independently in different parts of the world.

In the middle of the nineteenth century, Louis Pasteur published the scientific research on the formation of vinegar that is still relied on as a reference today. His findings paved the way for the process used in modern commercial vinegar production, which is far less labor intensive and time consuming than ancient practices. (Many would argue, however, that the time and labor devoted to making fine vinegars throughout history, and in the present, are what infuses them with their delicious flavors and much of their medicinal value.)

Anything that can be made into an alcoholic beverage containing up to 18 percent alcohol can be transformed into vinegar. Bacteria called *acetobacter aceti*, which exist naturally in the air we breathe, convert alcohol into *acetic acid*—the puckery, cleansing sourness that is the main characteristic of any variety of vinegar. The acetic acid content of vinegar in large part determines its uses and varies according to the raw material employed. Rice wine vinegar, for example, is quite mild and low enough in acidity to be considered sweet; it's perfectly good on its own as a salad dressing. Distilled vinegar is highly acidic and only suitable for pickling and for household and garden uses. The acidity of red wine, malt, balsamic, white wine, and apple cider vinegar lies between these two extremes.

Vinegar is mostly water and contains only 2 calories per tablespoon. It is completely fat free and very low in sodium. Vinegars made the old-fashioned way—which you'll learn about in an upcoming section—are rich in vitamins and minerals, as well as healthy enzymes and acids. Each spoonful of naturally fermented vinegar contains the nutrient bounty of the plants or fruits used to make it, including the trace elements potassium, phosphorus, magnesium, sulfur, iron, and calcium. The fermentation process adds enzymes and amino acids to the mix. It's widely believed, in fact, that this process is what endows vinegar with its many healing properties.

AS AMERICAN AS APPLE CIDER VINEGAR

Did you know that vinegar could be made from coconuts? That's what natives of the Philippines use. In Mexico, cactus fruits are the raw material for tequila, from which vinegar is made. Malaysians use pineapple. Other cultures use molasses, sorghum, honey, beets, potatoes, melons, or maple syrup. It's probably no surprise to you that cultures around the globe learned to make vinegar from whatever was most readily available in their environment. The abundance of apples in America explains why apple cider vinegar is the most American of the vinegars made today.

Hard (alcoholic) apple cider was one of the staples of early American settlers. When you buy apple juice from the market, it has been pasteurized—heated to 170 degrees Fahrenheit for ten minutes. This kills off any yeasts or bacteria in the juice. When apple juice is not pasteurized, these natural yeasts and bacteria ferment the juice, transforming it into hard cider. If that hard cider isn't consumed within two weeks of being exposed to the air, it will begin to turn to vinegar.

Hard cider is nothing like the apple cider found on American supermarket shelves. In fact, Americans are the only people who think of sweet, nonalcoholic juice when they hear the words *apple cider*. The rest of the world won't consider it cider unless it's been fermented into an alcoholic beverage. From now on, I'll refer to the typical supermarket cider or the fresh squeezings from apples as "sweet cider," to differentiate it from the tangy warmth of alcoholic hard cider.

Hard cider contains, on average, about 6 percent alcohol. This warming beverage probably helped early settlers to get through the long, chilly winters. In fact, in pioneer days hard cider was a winter provision as crucial as firewood and food.

Around 8,000 years ago, apples first appeared as a cultivated crop in Asia and Europe. Most likely, as soon as someone bit into an apple that had lain on the ground long enough to begin to ferment into alcohol, the seed for the idea of hard cider was planted. In the early 1300s, cider making hit its peak in England, and seventy-four of eighty parishes in West Sussex were paying their church tithes in cider. From the 1300s on, English workers in monastery orchards were paid partly in cider: 2 quarts a day for a grown man and 1 for a boy. (This practice was outlawed 500 years later.)

In the second and third centuries A.C.E., the term *sicera* was used to denote hard cider; this is where the modern word *cider* is believed to originate. *Sikera* is Greek for "intoxicating beverage" and comes from the Hebrew word *sekar*—thought by many to be the origin of the word *schnockered*, a word used today to describe the state of one who has had "a few too many."

The production and consumption of hard cider in the American colonies was nothing short of extraordinary. Records show that a single Massachusetts settlement of forty families put up 3,000 barrels for a single winter. By 1775, one out of every ten New England farms owned and operated its own cider mill, and it wasn't unusual for a town's residents to quaff 35 gallons per capita in a year's time. An apple grower in New Hampshire reportedly brewed 4,000 barrels one season, all of which were consumed by a nearby town before the next apple harvest.

Cider was valuable currency in the colonial barter economy, just as apples had been several millennia before in Asia and Europe. An 1805 diary reported one colonist's take on the tradition of giving apples to the teacher: the trading of a half-barrel of cider for a child's schooling. The north orchards of Thomas Jefferson's Monticello estate were dedicated to the production of fine cider, for which Jefferson reportedly preferred apples of the Virginia Hewes Crab and Golden Permian varieties. He wasn't the only president to value the constitutional benefits of hard cider: John Quincy Adams reputedly started off each day with a glassful of the hearty concoction.

In those days, the British had their beer and the French had their wine—and each enjoyed the vinegars made from those spirits. The Americans had their hard cider, and from it they made apple cider vinegar. As valuable a currency as hard cider was in the Colonies, cider vinegar was more so. At one time, the sale of cider vinegar was three times as profitable as the sale of hard cider.

Hard cider continued to be Americans' customary drink until the early nineteenth century. With the Industrial Revolution gaining momentum, more and more families abandoned their farms and apple orchards for life in the city. In 1899, 55 million gallons of cider were produced on U.S. farms; by 1919, the year Prohibition began, production had dwindled to only 13 million gallons. Some cider makers began to sell adulterated cider, cut with water or made with raw materials other than apples; this caused hard cider's reputation to deteriorate, and in some circles it was considered suitable only for poor drunkards.

When the temperance movement hit its stride, some activists took it on themselves to chop down apple orchards. Others served hard cider at temperance meetings, where tactics for ridding the states of demon rum, wild whiskey, and other distilled spirits were discussed. Despite its worsening reputation, cider was one of the few exemptions to the Volstead Act. Cider's popularity continued to diminish, however, and beer became a more popular alcoholic refreshment in the United States. Today, hard cider is beginning to make a comeback as a delicious and nutritious alcoholic beverage.

THE MAKING OF VINEGAR

Since the olden days, when vinegars were made at home simply by leaving alcoholic brews exposed to the air, the methods for making these tart, invigorating potions have evolved into somewhat of an art.

The *acetobacter* reaction is *aerobic,* meaning that it requires oxygen—the more oxygen, the better. To make vinegar, all you really need to do is expose some wine, beer, or cider to oxygen, while protecting it against opportunistic insects. Store it in a warm, dark place (the optimum temperature is about 85 degrees Fahrenheit) and wait; you'll end up with vinegar. Variations on this theme have yielded the varied methods for vinegar making known today.

In France, a nation well known for its culinary artistry, the *Orléans method* for vinegar making was developed in the year 1394. A group of French vintners, who had up until then viewed the transformation of their wines into vinegar as a liability, found that there was a lucrative market for their bad luck. They formed a guild of professional vinegar makers based in Orléans, France, called the Corporatif des Maîtres-Vinaigriers d'Orléans.

In the Orléans method, wooden barrels are laid on their sides, bung-holes up. A hole is drilled at each end, placed so that the barrel will be about three-fourths full when filled to just below the holes. The barrel is then filled to this point with beer, dilute wine, or cider, and a vinegar bacteria "starter" known as a *mother*. (If you've ever made sourdough bread or homemade yogurt, you've already had the experience of using a starter.) Vinegar mother consists of a thick layer of active *acetobacter*, and forms where the liquid has the most contact with oxygen.

Next, screening or cloth is used to cover the holes. After sitting for several months, the liquid transforms into vinegar, with a thick scum on the surface of the mash—the mother for the next batch. The vinegar is siphoned off through a spigot at the bottom of one end of the barrel, with about 15 percent left behind to "charge" the next batch. It's best not to break up the mother while this new batch is started, so more alcoholic liquid is added to the barrel through a long funnel pushed through the surface of the mother.

The development of faster, more modern methods has involved finding ways to expose more of the *acetobacter* to oxygen. A large container is loosely packed with porous material such as wood shavings, corncobs, or pomace (the pulp that remains after grapes or other fruits are pressed). The vinegar mother and liquid are then allowed to slowly trickle through, greatly increasing the rate at which *acetobacter* transforms alcohol into acetic acid. Fast methods allow volatile aromas to evaporate from the vinegar, while slower methods preserve more of the rich smells and tastes.

More recently—since 1952—an even faster method has been used: an aerator placed at the bottom of the vinegar generator suffuses the entire mash with tiny air bubbles. This technique can cut the time required to produce vinegar from months to days. The vinegars yielded by these quicker methods, however, do not have the same flavorful complexity or nutritional value found in vinegars made in the more traditional ways.

The most time-consuming and labor-intensive method for vinegar production is the old-world Solera Method. Vinegars made in this way are aged in wood, often for decades, and sometimes even in a succession of barrels made from different types of wood. Such vinegars are made from the best vintages of wine, are blended by expert practitioners of the vinegar-making art, and can cost as much as the finest wines.

TYPES OF VINEGAR

Apple Cider Vinegar

The best apple cider vinegars are made from fresh, whole, organic, sweet apples, ground to a pulp and cold-pressed to extract the juice. The juice is fermented to hard cider in one container, then transferred to another container with a vinegar mother to ferment to apple cider vinegar.

Cider vinegar adds a luscious tang to many foods. You can use it in sauces, marinades, even desserts. When you buy apple cider vinegar, don't be put off by sediment floating in the bottle; sediment is a sign that the vinegar is robust and full of nutrition. Less costly brands sacrifice taste and nutritional value, and you're far better off making the investment in fine brands or making your own from fresh apples. The best apple cider vinegar has a tart apple smell and a deep orange-brown color from the tannins found in fresh, ripe apples.

Buy fresh, organic apples from your local orchard, farmer's market, produce stand, or health food store. They don't need to be pristine for you to make cider vinegar from them; sometimes you can get a good deal on large quantities of apples that have been slightly bruised or pierced (although heavy bruising or brown, rotten spots is reason enough to pass them up). If you can't get your hands on any

What You Need to Make Your Own
Apple Cider Vinegar

To make the best possible apple cider vinegar from scratch, you'll
need the following:

- Apples (of course!)
- Wooden crates for apple storage
- A metal or plastic funnel
- An apple grinder (which you can get from one of the
  following organizations: Happy Valley Ranch in Paola,
  Kansas, at (913) 849-3103 or www.happyvalleyranch.com; or
  Lehman's Hardware at (330) 857-1111 or www.lehmans.com
- A cider press (which you can get from either of the
  above organizations; or try The Phoenix Foundry at
  (509) 684-5434
- A vessel for the first fermentation (a recycled gallon glass
  wine jug will do fine)
- A hydrometer (which you can get at a home-brewing store
  or Web site)
- A wooden barrel or cask, large ceramic crock, or food-grade
  plastic bucket for the second fermentation
- A vinegar "mother" (see page 13)
- Bottles for the final product

This type of vinegar has the greatest health-supporting benefits of
the vinegars described in these pages, but there are many other vinegars you can use to add flavor to your life and improve your health.

pesticide-free ones, be sure to wash apples thoroughly in a very mild bleach solution to rid them of chemicals, and rinse them carefully.

What type of apple is best? It depends on the result you want. There are over 1,100 native American apple varieties from which to choose. They are classified in three general categories: dessert apples, those that are best crunched into fresh off the tree; cooking apples; and cider apples. Cider blends often use apples from all three categories.

The list on page 12 shows all of the North American apples recommended for the making of cider and, therefore, the best-tasting cider vinegar. Mix and match any of these varieties. Try to achieve a balance between juicy sweetness, which yields a cider that keeps well and tastes delicious, and tartness, which counteracts sweetness and improves the cider's ability to resist discoloration and undesirable bacteria.

Red apples are usually sweeter than tart green varieties and will yield a stronger, more acidic vinegar (remember, the sugars are what turn into acetic acid). Tart apples will yield a sharper taste. It's preferable to use late-season apples—those that ripen around October or the time of the season's first frost. A bushel of apples (about 125 medium-sized ones) will make 2 to 3 gallons of cider.

The next thing you'll need to do is grind your apples. The purpose of this step is to make a uniform pulp that will allow the pressing to draw out as much juice as possible from each and every apple. First, be sure your apples are ripe; you can do so by cutting one in half and checking that the seeds are dark brown rather than greenish-tan. Rinse them in a large tub filled with cold, clean water, swirling them gently and draining them in a wicker or plastic laundry basket. Discard any apples that don't float. Next, pour whole apples into your grinder.

As you grind the apples, a wonderful-smelling, wet, golden mash called *pomace* will emerge. Use your apple cider press to separate the juice from the mash. Collect the juice in plastic or stainless steel

The Best Apples to
Use for Cider Vinegar

Ashmead's Kernel

Baldwin

Black Twig

Bramley's Seedling

Bullock

Cortland

Cox's Orange Pippin

Egremont Russet

Esopus Spitzenburg

Fameuse (Snow)

Freedom

Gilpin

Golden Harvey

Golden Russet

Golden Sweet

Granny Smith

Gravenstein

Grimes Golden

Haralson

Hewes (Virginia) Crab

Honey Cider

Jonathan

Jordan Russet

King David

McIntosh

Mutsu

Northern Pippin

Northern Spy

Red Delicious

Red June

Rhode Island Greening

Ribston Pippin

Rome Beauty

Roxbury Russet

Sops of Wine

St. Edmund's Pippin

Stayman Winesap

Tolman Sweet

Tompkins King (King)

Vandevere

Wagener

Wickson

Winesap

Winter Banana

York Imperial

Source: Ben Watson, *Cider: Hard And Sweet*, (Woodstock, VT, Country-man Press, 1999), 40–41.

containers, then strain it through cheesecloth into clean gallon jugs and seal tightly. Sip a cup of the fresh apple juice before continuing, if you like—mmm, good!

Allow the finished sweet cider to sit for twenty-four hours at room temperature. It will darken somewhat and become cloudy, and a gray deposit known as the *lees* will form on the bottom. Pour the cider into a new jug for fermentation, leaving the lees behind. Cover the new jug's neck with a small balloon. This will keep oxygen out of your cider, which is important for the work of the yeasts that ferment the sugars to alcohol. The balloon will expand as carbon dioxide is released from the cider.

In six or eight weeks, the cider will have done what comes naturally: the sugars will have fermented to alcohol. When it's done fermenting, it will contain lots of lees (at the bottom of the container), and the liquid will begin to look clearer. Skim off any grayish foam that has formed on the top of the cider—it's just extra yeasts—and transfer the cider into another clean container for the second fermentation, again leaving the lees behind.

To continue the process, you'll need a mother of vinegar. While the cider will probably turn to vinegar on its own if left to sit, you're taking a risk by letting just any old bacteria in the air do the work of souring this sweet liquid. You may be able to purchase a mother from a health food store. Some brands of organic apple cider vinegar—notably, the one made by Bragg's—come with some of the mother still floating inside.

If you can't find a mother of vinegar for sale, you can take your chances with natural *acetobacter* floating into the cider, or you can start your own. To make a mother of vinegar, pour some hard cider into a pint-sized jar and cover it with cheesecloth to keep out thirsty insects. Set it in a warm, dark place, where the temperature stays between 59 and 86 degrees Fahrenheit. In a few weeks' time, a sticky, stringy, sour-smelling layer of mother will form. You'll know it's ready by the pungent vinegar smell.

Apple Cider Vinegar Shortcuts

Here are a few traditional shortcuts used to make apple cider vinegar:

1. You can't make cider vinegar from store-bought apple juice. The preservatives and pasteurization suck the life out of the juice and it won't turn to vinegar. You can, however, try simply leaving fresh sweet cider standing in a jug covered with cheesecloth for four to six weeks. It will turn to vinegar, although its taste may leave much to be desired in comparison with cider vinegar made as described previously.
2. Cut up some apples and place into a stone crock. Cover them with warm water and cover the top of the crock with cheesecloth. After four to six months, strain off the vinegar. (A lump of raw bread dough will hurry things along.)
3. Collect apple and peach peelings and grape skins in a wide-mouthed jar. Cover them with cold water and set in a warm place, adding a couple of fresh apple cores every week or so. When scum forms on the top, stop adding fruit and just let it ferment and thicken for a few months. Strain through a cheesecloth when the taste seems right.

Be sure the mother doesn't get submerged in liquid. It has to stay afloat on the surface of the vinegar or the *acetobacter* will quite literally drown for lack of oxygen.

Concerned about bad bacteria growing in your cider as it undergoes fermentation? You don't need to be. While virulent *E.coli* strains can grow in sweet cider, something about the fermentation processes (to alcohol and to vinegar) makes hard cider and cider vinegar inhospitable places for such bacteria.

Once you have your vinegar mother, pour your hard cider into a wooden barrel, cask, or ceramic crock. Vinegar matured in wood

tastes and ferments better. Add the mother and cover the container
with several layers of cheesecloth or muslin to keep dust and insects
out. Make sure air can get through to the hard cider, and leave it in a
warm, dark place. It will take several months for the *acetobacter* in
the mother to transform the cider into tart cider vinegar. If you want to
keep the mother for future use, remove it when your vinegar tastes
about right; if it is left there after it consumes all of the alcohol in the
cider, it will die and sink to the bottom.

Balsamic Vinegar

Created in the province of Modena, Italy, this delectable vinegar has
been made since the Middle Ages. The Holy Roman Emperor Henry
III was given a barrel of balsamic vinegar in the year 1046, in honor
of his coronation. A touch sweet, a touch sour, dark, smooth, mellow,
and full of subtle, complex flavors, balsamic vinegar is unique among
vinegars in that it is made from unfermented grape juice.

Balsamic vinegar makers must have long experience and expertise
to time this process perfectly. Each master vinegar maker has his or
her own ways of shaping the final product, and the climate of the area
also contributes. The best balsamic vinegars are made from Treb-
biano or Lambrusco grape juice that has been slowly boiled almost to
the consistency of syrup. These grapes have a high sugar content
compared to other grapes. Grape juice must be boiled before fermentation to yield the distinctive balsamic flavor.

After boiling, the remaining concentrated syrup is cooled and
siphoned into a barrel that allows air to flow through. Yeasts in the air ferment a portion of the sugars into alcohol, but some of the sugars remain
as a residue. The resulting mix is then aged for three or more years, with
the best varieties aged in aromatic wood for at least twelve years. The
most outstanding balsamic vinegars are aged progressively in a series of
as many as seven different woods, but most use only three barrels: one of

oak, one of chestnut, and one of mulberry or juniper. Each wood imparts a unique layer of flavor to the finished product. Yearly, small amounts of new vinegar and cooked grape juice are added to the barrels; this prevents the formation of hard caramel along the inside of the containers. The vinegar is transferred from barrel to barrel according to each maker's techniques, diminishing in quantity with each transfer until the final precious elixir is sealed into a small wooden cask.

Look for a balsamic vinegar that is thicker than other vinegars and sweet in flavor, with a mahogany sheen. The acidity of balsamic vinegar is just enough to complement the flavors infused from the aromatic woods in which it has been aged. If you want to invest in the world's best—aged 50 to 200 years—plan to spend as much as you would for good cognac or a tin of caviar.

Fortunately for those of us who would rather spend less, relatively good balsamic vinegar can be made much more cheaply with modern methods. Any true balsamic vinegar, however, must be aged in wood for at least three years, according to Italian law. Look for a label that says "made in Modena, Italy," or "aged in wood," or "genuine basalmic vinegar." If these statements aren't on the label, you could be buying red wine cut with sugar and water.

Use balsamic vinegar in sauces, marinades, or salad dressings. Try dribbling a tablespoonful of good balsamic vinegar over a scoop of vanilla ice cream!

Wine Vinegar

This deep red variety is rich, mellow, and complex in flavor. The most delicious wine vinegars will state on their labels that they are made by the Orléans process or that they are aged in wood. Some labels will read "Vinaigre á l'ancienne." Good red wine vinegar is deep pink, lighter than red wine, while white wine vinegar is pale gold. The best wine

How to Make Your Own
Wine Vinegar

Start with a good-quality wine. Don't mix red and white wines together! Simply pour the wine into a crock or dark glass container. Add mother of vinegar, cover with a coarse cloth, and leave in a warm, airy spot for a few weeks, undisturbed. The best way to know whether it's done brewing is to taste it; it could take up to six months to fully mature. You can also make white wine vinegar by putting two pounds of raisins into a gallon of water and setting it in a warm area. After only a couple of months, you'll have a batch of white wine vinegar; strain it off and bottle it. You can make more by adding another half-pound of raisins and a gallon of water to the dredges.

vinegars are clear. Use wine vinegars for marinades (dark meats only), red sauces, or salad dressings, or for making fruit or herb vinegars.

Sherry Vinegar

The best sherry vinegars are made in the southwestern area of Spain. Made from the finest wines and matured in wood for twenty to thirty years, they are rich and mellow, with a stronger taste than red wine vinegar. Prime sherry vinegars cost more than wine vinegars but much less than the best balsamic vinegars. Many chefs regard sherry vinegar as an excellent value, useful for many delicious dishes, including marinated meats and poultry dishes and soups and sauces with a tomato base.

If you don't have sherry vinegar around the house and need some for a recipe, you can substitute a good white wine vinegar.

Whip Up a Red Wine and Olive Oil Vinaigrette

Here's a basic recipe you can use to make a healthy salad dressing:

Mix ½ cup of olive oil, 3 to 4 tablespoons of red wine vinegar, ½ teaspoon of Dijon mustard, and a dash of freshly ground pepper. Shake well before pouring over greens. You can keep this vinaigrette in the refrigerator for up to two weeks.

The vinegar isn't the only health-promoting ingredient in this dressing. Olive oil is an integral part of the Mediterranean diet, known to be one of the world's healthiest cuisines. The Mediterranean diet is rich in vegetables, fruits, and grains, and the main flesh food eaten is fish. Only very small amounts of red meat, sweets, or eggs are used. Wine is drunk in moderation, and olive oil is used instead of butter or other oils. Olive oil helps your body to resist heart disease and breast cancer, and won't become oxidized and cause free radical overload when heated, as oils pressed from nuts and seeds do.

Choose extra virgin olive oil for dressings. It's made from the highest quality olives and has a delicious, mellow flavor.

Champagne Vinegar

This delicate, smooth golden vinegar is as delicious as it sounds. Use it in poultry and seafood sauces.

Malt Vinegar

Made from malted, fermented barley, this type of vinegar was originally made by European breweries looking to dispose of beer that had gone bad. It has a very strong flavor, useful for pickling or as a condiment. In Europe, malt vinegar is a much more usual complement to thick-cut French fries ("chips") than ketchup. If this seems odd to you, keep in mind that ketchup contains vinegar.

To make malt vinegar, a mash of malted barley is heated with water and fermented into an unrefined beer called *gyle*. The gyle is then allowed to seep through wood shavings—often beechwood—in plastic or steel vats, into which a vinegar mother is placed. The resulting clear vinegar is filtered and aged, and is then colored with caramel to give it a golden, beerlike hue.

Old-fashioned mint sauce, used to accompany roasted lamb, is made with malt vinegar, as are some other recipes for flavorful relishes, chutneys, and salads (potato salad and coleslaw). Malt vinegar's hearty flavor comes at a lower price than that of wine vinegars.

Rice Vinegar

Red, black, and white varieties of rice vinegar are available. Rice vinegar has been made in China for more than 3,000 years, and it is an important ingredient in Japanese cuisine. The addition of rice vinegar to sushi rice has more than a culinary rationale: it is highly effective at killing dangerous pathogenic bacteria that may be found on raw fish, including *streptococcus* and *salmonella*.

Rice vinegar is made from rice wine, or *sake*. On the southern Japanese island of Kyushu, a unique 1,000-year-old method for making rice vinegar continues to be used today. The resultant black vinegar contains the nutrients found in the germ and bran of the rice, including a wide complement of essential amino acids. This Kyushu vinegar is expensive and widely appreciated for its medicinal value as well as its mild, sweet flavor.

Thick sake made from only brown rice and spring water is used to make this unique black vinegar. Sake is made by steaming brown rice and sprinkling it with spores of *aspergillus* mold. While incubating in a warm, humid room, the *aspergillus* grows and begins to produce digestive enzymes, drawing needed nutrients from the brown rice. Within two days this process yields *koji*, the starter used in many of the fermented foods enjoyed in Japanese cuisine. The koji is added to some more cooked brown rice and water, and this mixture is then poured into 100-gallon wooden casks.

Over the span of two months, the enzyme-rich koji breaks down the proteins, fats, and carbohydrates in the rice to amino acids, fatty acids, and simple sugars. Naturally occurring yeasts turn the sugars into alcohol, yielding the delicious rice wine known as sake. Once the alcohol content of the sake reaches about 20 percent, yeast growth is inhibited, and fermentation ceases. The sake is then ready to be mixed with spring water and "seed vinegar" from a previous batch. Once this has been done, the mixture is poured into earthenware crocks and sealed with thick natural-fiber paper and wooden lids.

Kyushu brown rice vinegar is the only commercially available natural rice vinegar that is made outdoors. The crocks, partially buried in the earth, are arranged in rows from north to south, for maximum exposure to the sun's warmth as it travels across the sky from east to west. Tall grass is allowed to grow around the crocks in the summer to prevent overheating, and in winter the grass is shorn low to expose more of the crocks' surface area to the sunshine. By burying the crocks two-thirds underground, the vinegar brewers maintain the temperature of their contents within a narrow range. Because the temperature range varies only slightly, the vinegar gains deep character and richness.

Naturally brewed rice vinegar is light and sweet—sweet enough to be used on its own as a dressing or seasoning. It's good for salad dressings, vegetable pickling, dips, sauces, and spreads, and its health benefits are touted throughout China and Japan.

Umeboshi Vinegar

This delectable, salty vinegar is made from fermented umeboshi plums. It's used in Oriental cuisine and can be used in recipes that require salt to cut down on the amount you'll need to add for good flavor.

Distilled White Vinegar

This clear vinegar is not naturally fermented. It is distilled from common grains and has been referred to as the "vodka of vinegars." Sharp and acidic, distilled vinegar is suitable only for pickling cucumbers, beans, and onions, or in strong sauces such as salsa where added flavor is unnecessary or undesirable. Its relatively high acid content (13 percent) and low price make white vinegar ideal for cleaning and other household, nonculinary uses.

YOU GET WHAT YOU PAY FOR

Cheap vinegars are generally watered down, overpasteurized, highly filtered, and overprocessed compared with pure, organic, aged-in-wood, unfiltered varieties. Read labels on wine vinegars, rice vinegars, and malt vinegars to be sure they have been made with care. (Of course, if you're using vinegar for household cleaning purposes, this doesn't apply.)

Make Your Own Infused Vinegar

To make your own infused vinegar, you'll need the following:

- a good wine vinegar, apple cider vinegar, or rice wine vinegar
- infusions of your choice, such as sweet berries or savory herbs
- an attractive bottle—try a wine or champagne bottle, or purchase elegant bottles that appeal to your eye
- a cork or other nonmetal stopper
- wooden skewers to poke infusions into an arrangement you like

Use your best judgment or some lively experimentation to determine the proportions of vinegar to infusion. I suggest you start off with a ratio of 1 pint to 4 tablespoons.

Your best bet for finding high-quality vinegar of any kind is to go to a specialty foods store or a health food store. If you have trouble finding vinegar that fits these descriptions, try making your own.

INFUSED VINEGAR HOW-TOS

Any delicate or neutrally flavored vinegar can be steeped with herbs, garlic, berries or other fruits, vegetables, or even flowers. These additions lend distinctive flavor and color to the vinegar. Bottled in clear glass bottles or jars, these vinegars are lovely to look at as well as delicious. They make terrific holiday gifts.

Herb-Infused Vinegars

You can make herb vinegars one of two ways. The technique preferred by experts is more time consuming and yields a stronger flavor, but the quick method is much easier and the finished product quite satisfactory. With the first method, bring the vinegar to a boil and add either fresh or dried herbs. Simmer for about half an hour and cool, strain, and bottle. Poke a few sprigs of fresh herbs into the bottle as garnish and identification, then seal with your nonmetal stopper.

To make herb vinegars with the second technique, wash and dry fresh herbs and tuck them into your bottle. Pour vinegar that is at room temperature or that has been gently warmed (this helps bring out the herbs' flavor) over the herbs. If you use warmed vinegar, allow it to cool before sealing. Stand the sealed bottles where they will be in the sunlight, and allow to stand for two weeks. Taste the vinegar to be sure it has the right flavor; if it doesn't, it may need more time to steep. Strain off the herbs if you like, or leave them in the bottle for a decorative touch.

Basil, thyme, rosemary, bay leaves, dill, tarragon, and lemon balm are good choices for infused vinegar. You can complement the flavors of the herbs with a clove of garlic (try this with basil) or a twist of orange or lemon peel (try this with rosemary). Herb vinegars can be used for dressings, pickling, casseroles, marinades, or sauces—anything that would include the herb that has been added to the vinegar.

Fruit Vinegars

Any fruit can be fermented into alcohol and then into vinegar, but you can infuse cider or white wine vinegar with the flavor, color, and nutrients of fresh fruit for a more complex taste and beautiful appearance.

Fruit vinegars were originally used as cordials. They were either warmed with a spoonful of honey to soothe a sore throat or served with cold water, ice, and sugar syrup as a refreshing drink for a hot summer's day. They're also tasty mixed with club soda or sparkling water, with a twist of lemon. You can use peaches, plums, cherries, or pears to make fruit vinegars, but my favorites are based on berries: raspberries, blackberries, strawberries, lightly crushed blueberries, and black and red currants all make refreshing, delicious fruit vinegars. Lately, research has shown that deeply hued berries are loaded with health-supporting, cancer-fighting phytonutrients, and teaming them up with the health benefits of vinegar is a one-two punch against ill health.

Raspberry Vinegar

2   pounds ripe raspberries
1   pint white wine or apple cider vinegar
1   pound sugar

In a glass bowl, combine raspberries and wine or vinegar. Allow to steep at least twenty-four hours, then press out the juice from the berries. Strain the liquid through cheese-cloth and add sugar. Pour into a nonmetallic pot and cook over moderate heat until the sugar dissolves. Bring to a boil and simmer until the mixture reaches the consistency of syrup. This recipe makes about 4 cups. To enjoy, sip it straight or mix it with water and ice in a tall glass.

Cherry Vinegar

1   cup pitted cherries
1   tablespoon sugar
1   pint warm red wine or apple cider vinegar

Rinse cherries and place them in a jar. Add sugar and pour wine or vinegar over the cherries. Seal the jar and allow it to stand about two weeks before straining and bottling. The recipe makes about 2 cups.

If you leave fruit in the bottle, it will probably fall apart after a while and may not be as attractive as you might like. If the look of the vinegar is important to you, strain the fruit out after steeping has blended its flavors with the vinegar base.

Fruit-infused vinegars add refinement to fruit salads and salad dressings. Or, try raspberry vinegar for basting or marinating lamb, plum vinegar for pork, or cherry vinegar with duck.

Floral Vinegars

Floral vinegars are a beautiful and tasty way to preserve the sense of summer all year long. Choose edible flowers such as roses, lavender, violet, marigold, nasturtium, primrose, or carnations. Check the petals of your harvest thoroughly for insect stowaways!

A high-quality white wine vinegar provides the perfect base. Adding a touch of honey will enhance the sweetness of the final product. Use about ¾ cup of flower heads to 2 cups of vinegar. Fill a jar halfway with clean, dry flowers, top off with vinegar, and seal the jar, allowing it to stand in a sunny spot for about two weeks. Check the taste; if it's weak, leave it a bit longer. Strain and bottle the floral vinegar when the flavor is just right. Add a fresh flower for garnish and identification.

When bottling infused vinegars for gift giving, spend time on presentation. Arrange the flowers or herbs with your wooden skewer until they're pleasing to the eye. Rather than sticking a label on, try tying dried flowers and handwritten tags around the neck of the bottle. Lay the bottle or bottles in a gift basket filled with long sprigs of the herb or flowers or whole, fresh pieces of the fruit you've used to infuse the vinegar. At the book's end, I'll give you recipes that include infused vinegars; if you decide to give one as a gift, a copy of a suitable recipe could be included in the gift basket. All in all, this is a great way to express your creativity and delight family and friends!

Pickles, Chutney, and Relishes

That brine that's left over in a pickle jar after you've consumed all of the crunchy pickles inside is vinegar. Pickling of vegetables is a traditional way to preserve their flavors and nutritional value; they keep quite well unrefrigerated for months, and in the days before refrigeration, pickling kept families eating vegetables through the long winters. A jar of pickled vegetables, chutney (a type of tart, tangy preserves), or relish also makes a great homemade gift for friends or family—or a lovely addition to your own pantry. Here are some recipes to get you started.

Spiced Pickling Vinegar

This vinegar is a good base for vegetable pickling or for making chutneys.

- 2 cinnamon sticks
- 2 blades of mace
- 4 teaspoons whole cloves
- 4 teaspoons allspice berries
- 1 tablespoon black peppercorns
- 4 cups apple cider vinegar

Divide the cinnamon, mace, cloves, allspice, and peppercorns equally between two sterilized bottles. Pour in vinegar to within ⅛ inch of the tops of the bottles. Seal the bottles and shake well, and keep them in a cool, dark place for two months before using. Shake them occasionally during this time to help the flavors blend and develop.

If you want to use your spiced vinegar sooner, heat the vinegar to just below boiling before pouring it into the bottles, then store it for a week.

*Mixed Vegetable Pickles**

1	pound green beans
1	pound small pickling onions
1	small cauliflower
12	ounces zucchini
8	ounces peeled carrots
½	cup sea salt
1¾	cups strained spiced pickling vinegar

Trim the beans and cut them into neat, 1-inch lengths. Trim and peel the onions, leaving a small length of root so that they do not fall apart. Cut the cauliflower into florets and break them into ½-inch pieces. Trim the zucchini and carrots and cut them into ⅛-inch-thick slices.

Layer the vegetables with the salt in a large glass or plastic bowl; put a plate on top to press moisture out of the vegetables. Leave for 24 to 48 hours. Then rinse the vegetables under cold water in a plastic sieve or colander, washing all the salt away. Drain the vegetables well and dry them on paper towels.

Pack vegetables in layers in sterilized Mason jars. Leave 1 inch of space at the top of each jar. Pour in the pickling vinegar to cover by ½ inch. Tap jars gently to remove air pockets, seal,

---

*Pickle, chutney, and relish recipes are from *Clearly Delicious: An Illustrated Guide to Preserving, Pickling, and Bottling*, by Elizabeth Lambert Ortiz (London, England: Carroll & Brown Limited, 1994).

and label. Keep the jars in a cool, dark place for at least six weeks.

Red Tomato Chutney

This easy-to-make chutney is a good addition to crusty, fresh bread and aged cheese—a delicious treat to enjoy with a glass of red wine while entertaining. This recipe makes about 6 cups of chutney.

3	pounds ripe tomatoes
1½	small onions
2	pounds cooking apples
2	cups white wine vinegar
½	cup sugar
1	cup raisins
2	teaspoons salt
1	teaspoon ground cloves
1	teaspoon ground ginger
½	teaspoon ground cayenne pepper

Core tomatoes and put in a bowl; cover with boiling water. Leave them in for 15 to 20 seconds, until the skins start to split. Transfer the tomatoes to a bowl of cold water. Remove from water one at a time and peel away skin with a sharp knife. Roughly chop the tomatoes.

Peel and thinly slice onions; peel, core, and chop apples. Put tomatoes, onions, and apples into a preserving pan (a wide, shallow pan made of stainless steel; don't use brass or copper). Add the remaining ingredients and stir to combine.

Bring the ingredients to a boil, stirring; then lower the heat and simmer for 40 to 45 minutes, stirring often. When done, the fruit and vegetables will be soft and the chutney will be reduced and thickened. Test by running the back of the spoon along the bottom of the pan—no runny liquid should be visible.

Spoon chutney into warmed, sterilized jars to within ⅛ inch of the tops. Stir to remove air pockets, seal the jars, and label. Allow jars to sit in a cool, dark place for two months.

Corn Relish

This relish makes a great side dish for summer picnics and barbecues.

8	ears fresh corn
2	each of red bell peppers, green bell peppers, and onions
8	ribs celery
4½	cups cider vinegar
½	cup sugar
1	tablespoon mustard seeds
1	tablespoon salt
4	allspice berries

Husk corn and remove silks. Cut the kernels off each cob. Cut around the core of each bell pepper, then pull the core out, halve each pepper lengthwise, and scrape out the seeds. Cut away the white ribs on the insides of the peppers, and then dice the peppers. Peel and finely chop the onions and finely chop the celery, then put all the ingredients into a preserving pan. Add all the remaining ingredients and stir over low heat until the sugar is completely dissolved. Bring the mixture to a boil, stirring, and simmer (stirring occasionally) for 15 to 20 minutes until vegetables are tender.

Spoon into warmed, sterilized jars to within ⅛ inch of the tops, seal the jars, and label. The relish can be used right away, but it will keep for several months.

Chapter Two

MEDICINE CABINET MIRACLES

Vim and Vinegar from Head to Toe

It's been known since antiquity that fruits, vegetables, and whole grains support good health. It was said in medieval England that "to eat an apple before going to bed/Will make the doctor beg his bread." In other words, an apple a day keeps the doctor away!

People have made cider, wine, and vinegars from these foods for many centuries in an effort to preserve and increase their utility, taste, and health benefits. When healthy foods are transformed into vinegar, they retain much of their nutrient bounty while gaining antiseptic, detoxifying, anti-inflammatory, pH-balancing, digestion-supporting, and infection-fighting qualities.

Today, with the advent of modern research techniques, we know more than ever before about *why* these foods are so good for us. Grapes, apples, and unrefined rice are packed with vitamins, minerals, healthful phytonutrients (plant chemicals), and fiber. Wine—especially red wine—has been intently studied for its disease-preventing actions. White wine vinegar possesses unique nutritional qualities, and rice wine vinegar is considered to be medicinal in many parts of Asia.

Apple cider vinegar is a versatile home remedy that has been passed down through generations. It's so versatile, in fact, that some might believe its many uses to be the fabrication of snake-oil salesmen. The best way to know for yourself is to try some of the uses I'll recommend in the rest of this book. There's certainly no risk, as vinegar is about as nontoxic as a remedy can be.

In this chapter, you'll learn about the apple, from which the most medicinal of the vinegars is derived. You'll discover fascinating facts about its nutritional properties and disease-preventing potential. I'll also tell you about the unique properties of the vinegar made from apples, and about its beneficial effects when used internally and externally.

Other vinegars—most notably, those made from grapes and rice—also have health-promoting qualities. Vinegars made from red grapes show particular promise, because they contain the same cancer-preventive, circulation-supporting plant chemicals that have put red wine in the health headlines for some years now. I'll tell you about a number of uses for these vinegars as well.

ALL ABOUT APPLES

When the Pilgrims arrived in America, they found crabapple trees waiting for them. These tough, sour little morsels didn't agree too well with their taste buds in comparison with the big, sweet, juicy apples they'd left behind in England. The Massachusetts Bay Colony requested that those on later voyages of the *Mayflower* bring along seeds and cuttings so that more appetizing fruit could be cultivated. Others immigrating to the United States from Europe did so as well. John Chapman, a fellow from Massachusetts, gained a place in history for planting apple trees throughout Indiana, Illinois, and Ohio; you probably know him as Johnny Appleseed.

Over half of the U.S. apple crop is produced in the state of Washington, where over 12 billion apples are picked by hand each year. Cultivated apples grown from seed rarely, if ever, resemble their parents. Seeds from sour apples can yield sweet varieties; seeds from red apples can yield yellow or green varieties; the seeds of large apples can yield small ones. To cultivate a single apple variety consistently, a grower must use grafting techniques—essentially, the cloning of trees. Apple cultivation is a complicated science and a rewarding art.

A full-sized apple tree can grow to four stories in height and spread over 1,600 square feet. One tree can easily yield 10 or more bushels of apples. One bushel of apples contains approximately 125 medium-sized fruits—enough to make fifteen 9-inch pies, thirty-six pint jars of applesauce, or 2 to 3 gallons of cider. If you'd like to grow an apple tree but don't have space for such an enormous plant, you'll be glad to know that dwarf hybrids grow only 6 to 12 feet tall and spread over less than 150 square feet. These little trees produce full-sized apples that are every bit as delicious as those on the larger trees.

The average American eats roughly 19.6 pounds of apples per year. About half of the apples grown in the U.S. are sold fresh, with the other 50 percent going toward the making of apple juice, applesauce, apple pie filling, or canned apples.

The typical apple weighs approximately 150 grams (5 ounces) and contains about 100 calories, 18 grams of carbohydrate, 2.3 grams of fiber, and almost no fat or protein. Most of the fiber in apples is soluble, and soluble fiber may aid those who wish to lower high blood cholesterol levels. Apples are a good source of vitamins and minerals, with 10 mg of vitamin C, 150 IU of vitamin A, and small but significant amounts of several B vitamins. Each apple you crunch into also contains 159 mg of potassium, 15 mg each of calcium, magnesium, and phosphorus, and 0.5 mg iron. Apples also contain trace amounts of manganese, copper, selenium, and zinc.

The health benefits of eating apples have been known since antiquity, but only recently has modern science discovered exactly how compounds in apples support wellness. This modern research might translate roughly to: "a dose of antioxidant flavonoids and polyphenols, soluble fiber, vitamins, and minerals a day keeps the doctor away." Flavonoids and polyphenols are chemical compounds found in the colorful portions of fruits and vegetables, and their effects in preventing cancer and heart disease have been studied extensively in recent years.

According to scientists at Cornell University, a single apple contains more antioxidant power than 1,500 mg of vitamin C. (You'll learn more about the wonders of antioxidant nutrients later in this chapter.)

Two apples a day—or an apple and some apple cider vinegar—can also help to stave off osteoporosis. Each apple contains 1 mg of the mineral boron, which is thought to prevent bone mineral loss.

APPLE CIDER VINEGAR'S BOUNTY

Apple cider vinegar is a concentrated nutrient powerhouse that contains flavonoids, polyphenols, pectin, and enzymes and amino acids that form during fermentation. Its contents include the following.

Acids

The acetic acid, isobutyric acid, lactic acid, and propionic acid contained in apple cider vinegar can do wonders for your digestion and your acid/alkaline balance (you'll find out how as you read on). These healthy acids also help control the growth of unwelcome bacteria and yeasts throughout your body. It's believed that acids in vinegar have a purifying and detoxifying effect; one study from researchers at Massachusetts General Hospital found that acetic acid binds to one type of antibiotic, transforming it into a form that is more easily eliminated from the body.

Amino Acids

These are the building blocks of protein. The amino acid content of vinegar depends on what it is made from. Some amino acids found in vinegar have antioxidant effects.

Beta-Carotene

Foods rich in this vitamin help prevent cancer and protect the body against damage caused by exposure to chemical toxins.

Boron and Other Bone-Building Minerals

Boron is found abundantly in fresh apples, and new research is showing that it works alongside calcium, magnesium, and phosphorus (all of which are found in apple cider vinegar as well) to build strong, dense bones.

Enzymes

Enzymes have many duties throughout the body. Built from protein molecules, they are indispensable for the inner workings of each and every cell. They are also employed during the process of digestion to break down foods as they pass through the small intestines. Your body can make enzymes to do this work, but many people find that they suffer from indigestion, gas, or bloating because they aren't making enough of these specialized digestive enzymes.

Fresh, raw foods such as apples are loaded with enzymes that aid in digestion. When sweet cider undergoes the double fermentation process that transforms it into vinegar, its enzyme bounty is strengthened.

Magnesium

This mineral is needed for so many cellular functions that several medical journals are devoted entirely to its study. The typical modern American diet is sorely lacking in magnesium; it's found most abundantly in fresh, unprocessed foods such as vegetables, fruits, and grains. Every 3½ ounces of apple cider vinegar contains 22 mg of easily absorbable magnesium.

Potassium

Processed foods are also stripped of this mineral, and usually sodium is added to these foods to give them the taste they lose during processing. In the typical American diet, the ratio of potassium to sodium (salt) is about 1 to 2. The ideal ratio is closer to 5 to 1. To make matters worse, most Americans further deplete their potassium stores by overdosing on caffeine and sugar—both of which act as diuretics, flushing water and minerals such as potassium out of the body. A balanced potassium-to-sodium ratio ensures that the muscles, including the heart muscle and the muscles that line the blood vessels, can contract and relax properly.

Apple cider vinegar is an excellent source of easily absorbable potassium: 100 mg per 3½ ounces. Making fruit vinegars with potassium-rich fresh berries or apricots will yield even more of this needed mineral.

Pectin

A type of soluble fiber, pectin can absorb water, toxins, and cholesterol in the digestive tract, improving both heart health and "regularity."

Tannins

When the cell walls of apples rupture during cider pressing, they release these red-gold plant chemicals—the same chemicals that lend color to autumn leaves. Tannins give fruits, vegetables, black tea, beer, and wine their characteristic astringent taste. They are effective antioxidants that help to prevent spoilage.

As-Yet-Unidentified Products of Fermentation

During the fermentation process, many new plant chemicals are created. No one has yet studied these chemicals to find out exactly what they are or how they might help stave off disease. In the future, I expect we'll discover that these fermentation products explain some of apple cider vinegar's miraculous healing effects.

Here's the complete nutrient breakdown for 3½ ounces of apple cider vinegar:

95 percent water
14 calories
zero protein or fat
5 grams carbohydrate
6 mg calcium
9 mg phosphorus
0.6 mg iron
1 mg sodium
100 mg potassium
22 mg magnesium
0.04 mg copper

INTERNAL BENEFITS OF VINEGAR

IMPORTANT! Whenever you take vinegar by mouth, be sure to rinse with clean, pure water afterward. Otherwise, the acids vinegar contains could eventually begin to erode the enamel on your teeth.

A Daily Health Tonic

Want to take a pure, natural multivitamin every morning to start your day off right? Drop 1 or 2 tablespoons of apple cider vinegar into a glass of clean, pure water and drink it down first thing in the morning. Feel free to add a teaspoon of honey. Sip your tonic as you would a cup of coffee or tea, and know that you're taking a positive step toward supplanting nutrient deficiencies that result from a diet containing processed, refined foods.

Aching Feet

Here's a fun folk remedy for feet that ache at the end of a long day: run a warm, ankle-deep bath and add ½ cup of apple cider vinegar. Walk back and forth in the tub for five minutes to get the blood circulating, which will help flush toxins out as the vinegar and water soothe and nourish.

Acid/Alkaline Balance

Most anything with a sour taste contains acid, and vinegar is certainly no exception to this rule. Acid is the opposite of *alkaline,* or "basic." Basic substances such as baking soda are soapy to the touch. Acidity and alkalinity are measured on the pH scale, which ranges from 1 (the most acidic) to 14 (the most basic). Neutral pH is 7, and acids are substances with a pH below 7. Vinegar's pH is right around 2.

Your bloodstream's pH stays right between 7.35 and 7.45— slightly on the alkaline side. Maintenance of proper pH is very important for optimal health; in fact, if it strays too far to either end of normal, serious illness and even death can result. Enzymes, microscopic workers that do crucial jobs within every cell, require the right pH to do their jobs, and they are shut down when pH shifts far out of the normal range. Fortunately, your organs have many "fail-safe" mechanisms for keeping pH within narrow limits.

What you choose to eat has a significant effect on pH. Generally, meats, dairy products, and refined sugar produce acid in your body, while most vegetables produce alkaline. This doesn't mean that eating too many acidic or alkaline foods will seriously hurt or kill you— again, you've got plenty of fail-safe mechanisms in your respiratory system and kidneys to balance things out, no matter what you eat. Many experts believe, however, that *subtle* shifts into more acidic pH within the body contribute to causing and worsening chronic health conditions and make the body a better host for all kinds of disease.

How does the body alkalinize itself? It does this by creating *bicarbonate ions,* which buffer (neutralize) acids. In response to acidic foods, your pancreas makes bicarbonate ions, which alkalinize the body by neutralizing those acids. This explains how vinegar helps your body to become more alkaline. Many natural health practitioners advise the use of cider vinegar tonics to help patients achieve pH balance in their bloodstreams.

Arthritis Help

Arthritis is one of the most common chronic diseases of aging in the Western world. Most arthritics suffer from *osteoarthritis,* where joints become worn down and painful. Over time, inflammation and permanent joint damage can result. As cartilage is worn away from joints, the body may try to fix the damage by depositing calcium, but often such calcium deposits create painful bone spurs that further compromise joint function.

People who are obese, avoid exercise, smoke, or shun vegetables are at greatly increased risk of developing arthritis. Conventional drug treatment—with painkillers, anti-inflammatories, and cortisone shots—sometimes works to relieve the symptoms but doesn't go to the root of the problem.

Some researchers have presented compelling evidence that osteoarthritis is caused in part by a buildup of irritant metabolic wastes and toxins in the joint tissues. Levels of these toxins and wastes can be reduced dramatically with the right diet choices, which I'll reveal to you in detail in Chapter 5 of this book. Some people will need to also identify and eliminate food allergens, most commonly foods containing wheat, dairy, corn, or citrus. Others will respond well to a diet free of *nightshade* vegetables, including tomatoes, eggplants, and summer squash. Nightshade vegetables contain plant chemicals that, in some sensitive people, cause or aggravate painful joints. It's also important to get some exercise, with the help of a physical therapist if necessary, and to shed excess pounds that might be putting too much stress on the joints.

Nutrient-rich apple cider vinegar can play a role in relieving pain and slowing the progression of arthritis. Its acids detoxify the body by binding to toxins and wastes, neutralizing them so that they can't do harm to body tissues. It's said that apple cider vinegar helps remove built-up calcium deposits from the joints. Take a vinegar tonic four times daily, containing 1 teaspoon of vinegar in a glass of water, with honey if you like. Another recipe to try:

Vinegar Tonic

2   stalks celery
½   grapefruit
1   orange
1   lemon

Cut up all ingredients (washed and unpeeled). Simmer in 4 cups of water, uncovered, for 1 hour. Press the softened fruits through a jelly bag or cheesecloth; stir in 1 tablespoon of apple cider vinegar and 1 tablespoon of Epsom salts (very high in magnesium, an essential and often-deficient mineral). Drink a full cup of water with a ¼ cup of this mixture each morning and evening. Within a month, you should begin to experience relief.

You can also rub down arthritic joints with a liniment made of two egg whites, ½ cup vinegar, and ¼ cup olive oil.

Asthma Relief

According to some practitioners of alternative medicine, the chest tightness and wheezing of asthma can be relieved with a special acupressure treatment that includes apple cider vinegar. Soak gauze pads in vinegar, then press them against the insides of both wrists. Wrap tape around the wrists to hold the pads in place.

You can also try a warm apple cider vinegar compress when breathing is difficult. Place a thin cloth soaked in apple cider vinegar over your throat and cover it with plastic wrap. Add a heating pad, towel moistened with hot water, or hot-water bottle. Lie in a comfortable position until breathing feels easier.

Bed-Wetting and Urinary Incontinence

Some experts believe that those who need to urinate frequently are doing so because of a pH imbalance. Urination is one way the body adjusts its pH balance, flushing away excess acids. A vinegar tonic before bed could help those who habitually wet their beds—or who suffer from stress incontinence—by improving their acid/alkaline balance.

Blood Pressure and Heart Health

Keeping blood pressure under control is an important part of preventing heart attacks and strokes. Dietary modifications (low to no salt, low saturated fats and hydrogenated fats, moderate coffee and alcohol) and apple cider vinegar tonics several times daily have been shown to lower blood pressure and strengthen the heart muscle.

There is some evidence that vinegar acts as a blood thinner, reducing the risk of blood clots that can clog vessels to the heart and in the brain. The potassium in apple cider vinegar helps to balance out sodium levels in the body, maintaining proper fluid balance; this helps to ensure that blood pressure stays within healthy limits. A dose of 2 tablespoons of vinegar and 2 tablespoons of honey in a glass of water with breakfast each day is believed to normalize blood pressure while lowering cholesterol.

Magnesium, another mineral found in apple cider vinegar, works to relax blood vessel walls, helping to normalize high blood pressure.

Bone Health

Trace minerals necessary for bone building include manganese, magnesium, phosphorus, calcium, and silicon. All of these minerals are found in apple cider vinegar, which delivers these minerals to the body in naturally balanced, easily absorbed forms.

I advise all of my readers to use a high-quality calcium supplement to ensure adequate levels of this mineral. With calcium supplementation, weight-bearing aerobic exercise (such as walking or jogging), and some type of strength training (such as lifting light weights or doing push-ups), bones can stay strong and resilient into old age.

The best source of supplemental calcium is a form called *calcium citrate*. This type of calcium is naturally bound to another substance that makes it more easily absorbed into the body. You can make your own calcium citrate supplements cheaply and easily from eggshells, and you'll get them along with the benefits of apple cider vinegar! Here's how: Wash eggshells and let them dry, then place in enough vinegar to cover. They will dissolve completely into the vinegar. Take a tablespoon or two of this mixture each day, mixed with water or juice.

If you choose to buy calcium supplements instead, you can use vinegar to find out whether they are being properly broken down and absorbed by your body. Drop a tablet into 3 ounces of room-temperature vinegar. Stir it briskly every five minutes for a half-hour. If the tablet hasn't completely disintegrated in this period of time, your body isn't able to make use of the calcium these tablets contain. (You can actually do this test with any vitamin or mineral supplement to see whether your body is able to break it down and absorb its contents.)

Cancer Prevention

To some degree, cancer is a symptom of the harm caused by free radicals. Free radicals are natural by-products of metabolism that are usually controlled by the antioxidant substances made in the cells or taken in through the diet. If antioxidants aren't plentiful enough to handle the free radical load, free radicals spill over, wreaking havoc throughout the body. When free radicals damage cells, they can cause changes in genetic material that lead to that cell becoming cancerous. This is one of the ways in which a diet rich in antioxidants protects against cancer.

Two researchers from Cornell University in New York State, Rui Hai Liu and Chang Yong Lee, have discovered that plant chemicals—*phytochemicals*—found in apples are protective against cancer formation. It has long been known that antioxidant nutrients found in apples, such as vitamin C and beta-carotene, are helpful in this regard. The research of Drs. Liu and Lee, however, has shown that phytochemicals such as *flavonoids* and *polyphenols* are equally important. They looked at the effects of an extract from apple skins on liver and colon cancer and found that growth of these cancers was slowed by 57 percent and 43 percent, respectively. The study concluded that only 100 grams of apple (the average apple weighs 150 grams, about 5 ounces) have the same antioxidant activity as 1,500 mg of vitamin C.

If you don't want to or can't eat an apple a day, you can make up for it with your daily dose of apple cider vinegar. When it's made with whole, fresh apples, apple cider vinegar retains the healthful properties found in the original apples.

Apple cider vinegar also contains beta-carotene, a powerful antioxidant. Moreover, carotenoids serve as the body's raw materials for the production of vitamin A, another potent antioxidant. Lack of vitamin A has been linked to cancers of the respiratory system, colon, and bladder. Carotenoids and vitamin A work in concert to protect the body from cancers associated with chemical toxins.

The American Cancer Society recommends a high-fiber diet for the prevention of colon cancer. According to a study in the *Journal of the National Cancer Institute*, pectin, a soluble fiber found in vinegar, binds certain cancer-causing compounds in the colon, speeding their elimination from the body.

A group of Western Michigan University researchers has reported test results that indicate vinegar can be used to increase the accuracy of conventional tests for cervical cancer. Adding the new vinegar-based test to the standard Pap test allows medical personnel to "detect women at risk for cervical cancer who would not have been

Red Wine Vinegar for Cancer Prevention

You've no doubt heard that red wine, drunk in moderation, seems to help people live longer, healthier lives. Red wine contains various antioxidant nutrients that have had potent anticancer action in both test-tube and animal studies. Many of these chemicals also help to prevent LDL oxidation (see page 46 for more on this), which is known to increase the risk of heart disease. Quercetin, resveratrol, catechins, and proanthocyanidins are but a few of these miraculous, health-supporting phytochemicals. It makes sense that including vinegars made from red grapes—such as balsamic and red wine vinegars—could help to protect you against cancer and heart disease.

detected by the Pap test alone." The vinegar test is simple to administer, noninvasive, safe, and low cost.

Cholesterol Control

High "bad" LDL blood cholesterol levels and low "good" HDL blood cholesterol levels are symptoms of blood vessel disease that can lead to clogged heart or brain arteries, heart attack, and stroke. While the evidence that unhealthy cholesterol counts *cause* these problems is far from conclusive—despite what conventional medicine has led you to believe—they do serve as an early warning that your risk of heart attack is on the rise. When cholesterol counts fall back into their proper balance due to changes in diet and exercise habits, you can feel confident that you're also improving your chances of avoiding heart attack and stroke.

Here are the lifestyle changes that bring cholesterol levels into balance: maintaining your ideal weight; getting daily or near-daily exercise; and replacing processed foods full of hydrogenated oils, sugars, and other unhealthy fats with vegetables and fruits. One of the reasons for adding more fresh, whole foods to your diet to lower cholesterol is that these foods are rich in fiber.

Fiber is the indigestible portion of foods. All fiber has beneficial effects on cholesterol counts, but not all fiber achieves this end in the same way. Some are *water soluble*, while others are not. *Insoluble* fiber can't be absorbed and passes right through the intestines and out with bowel movements, acting like a broom that sweeps wastes out easily.

Water-soluble fiber, such as the pectins found in apple cider vinegar made from whole fresh apples, binds to cholesterol in the digestive tract, preventing it from being absorbed into the body. Water-soluble fiber also adds bulk to bowel movements by holding water.

"Bad" LDL cholesterol can become *oxidized* in the body if it is attacked by free radicals. It's widely believed that these oxidized LDL molecules are one of the most harmful components of blood cholesterol; they can do damage to artery walls and begin the process that leads to clogged vessels. Amino acids and antioxidant phytochemicals found in apple cider vinegar have the power to neutralize this harmful form of LDL cholesterol.

Cold Care

Here's a great folk remedy to try the next time you have a chest cold. Soak an 8-inch square of brown paper (you can cut it from a paper grocery bag) in apple cider vinegar. When it's saturated, sprinkle on some pepper and bind it pepper side down over your chest. Use strips of cloth to secure the vinegar-soaked paper in place. Remove the paper after relaxing and breathing deeply for twenty minutes. You can also try the remedy I described for asthma on page 41 for chest colds.

Singers are especially careful not to catch colds, because of the havoc they can wreak on vocal chords. Some swear by an apple cider

---

High-Calcium Chicken Soup

To make a soup that fights off colds and is rich in easily absorbed calcium, follow this recipe from Emily Thacker's *The Vinegar Book.* (The parenthetical additions are mine.)

Simmer 2 to 3 pounds of chicken bones (organic, free-range chickens are best) uncovered for about 2 hours, in a gallon of water containing at least ½ cup of vinegar. The vinegar will leach calcium from the bones and enrich the broth. Strain the broth and skim off the fat; strip the meat from the bones to add to the broth. Discard the bones. Then add ¾ cup of tiny pasta, such as orzo. (If you'd rather use a whole grain such as rice, you can do so; cook the grain separately and add it to the broth.) Also add two bouillion cubes—choose natural ones that don't contain MSG—and bring the mixture to a boil and cook for 10 minutes. Remove from heat and dribble in two slightly beaten egg whites. Sprinkle 2 tablespoons of chopped parsley on top just before serving.

---

vinegar gargle of 1 teaspoon apple cider vinegar to ½ cup water to kill off bacteria and rinse away mucus.

Constipation

Constipation is a very common complaint among people who eat few vegetables and fruits and lots of processed foods. When fiber intake is low, the bowels can't move regularly. Also, normal digestion requires the production of acids and the enzyme *pepsin* by the stomach, as well as other enzymes from the pancreas. As we age, many of us begin to underproduce these digestive acids and enzymes. This can lead to all kinds of uncomfortable symptoms, not the least of which is constipation.

Eat your vegetables and fruits, and add pectin from apple cider vinegar to your diet. Try preparing a vegetable stir-fry with apple cider vinegar and olive oil, or making a healthy salad dressing from apple cider vinegar and olive oil.

Patricia Bragg, N.D., suggests the following recipe to get bowels moving: Boil 2 cups of distilled water and add 2 tablespoons of flaxseeds. Boil for ten more minutes before straining off the seeds. A jellylike liquid will be left behind. Drink a cup of this mixture with a teaspoon of apple cider vinegar. Or, you can simply add a tablespoon or two of psyllium powder to your apple cider vinegar cocktail.

Cough Remedy

Folk medicine holds that a sprinkle of apple cider vinegar on your pillowcase will soothe a dry night cough. Maybe you'd like to sleep on that!

Cramps

I've known many people who are often rudely awakened during the night by the sharp pain of muscle cramps. In most cases the pains occur in the legs, but they have been known to strike in the vicinity of the stomach or heart, which can be downright scary!

If you've ever had this type of cramp, you know the routine: jump out of bed and do whatever you have to do to work out the cramp. Pounding on the cramped area or "walking it out" usually will do the trick, but then you face the challenge of getting back to sleep, not knowing whether another excruciating cramp will awaken you again. Drinking down a glass of water with 1 or 2 tablespoons of apple cider vinegar and a touch of honey can help to prevent recurrences. You can also try the following mixture to keep nighttime cramps at bay: a teaspoon of honey, a teaspoon of apple cider vinegar, and a tablespoon of calcium lactate powder (which you should be able to purchase at a health food store or online), stirred into ½ cup of water. Drink this mixture once a day.

Depression

Eastern medicine practitioners believe that vinegar relieves stasis and stagnation. It's thought that vinegar gets the blood moving and circulating and that it helps to cleanse toxins from the liver. According to the Eastern medical model, depression may be experienced in the mind but is rooted in a stagnant liver. Others attribute vinegar's antidepressant effects to its energizing amino acid content. For mild depression, sip ⅓ cup of water with a teaspoon of apple cider vinegar three times daily.

Diabetes

In most individuals with diabetes, some level of digestive impairment is present. This includes underproduction of hydrochloric acid and protein-digesting pepsin in the stomach and the underproduction of digestive enzymes by the pancreas. Food is not completely broken down and absorbed, and the body gets insufficient nourishment; a person with diabetes may also experience constipation, gas, or diarrhea.

Apple cider vinegar's enzymes and acids promote better digestion in diabetics and others (see below). The pectin it contains has been shown to help control blood sugar levels in diabetics. In a study published in the *European Journal of Clinical Nutrition*, scientists found that a salad dressing that includes vinegar helps to stabilize blood glucose levels.

Diarrhea

Pectin provides antidiarrhea action, swelling to add bulk to watery stool. Intestinal bacteria transform pectin into a protective coating for the irritated intestinal lining, soothing the spasms that cause diarrhea. In addition, pectin is an effective antidote against several types of diarrhea-causing bacteria. It's potent stuff!

Ever used Kaopectate to treat a nasty bout of diarrhea? The "pectate" part of this over-the-counter diarrhea preparation is actually pectin. Save money and go natural by using apple cider vinegar instead.

Dietary Transition

People in the process of switching from a refined food and/or meat-centered diet to one primarily composed of whole grains and vegetables will benefit from taking a little vinegar. It will help the body manage the detoxification process that occurs during such a dietary shift and will support the digestive system as it deals with new foods. Sip ⅓ cup of water with 1 teaspoon of apple cider vinegar mixed in, three times daily.

If you're in the habit of avoiding highly nutritious legumes (beans) because of the gas they produce in your body, try adding vinegar to the soak water; ⅛ cup to ¼ cup of apple cider vinegar should do the trick. Once you've rinsed the beans after soaking, add some more vinegar to the cooking water. This essentially predigests some of the fiber that your body may not be able to handle on its own.

Digestive Health

In people over the age of fifty, it's quite common for hydrochloric acid (HCl) production in the stomach to be deficient. Low HCl production leads to many digestive problems. When your stomach is digesting a meal, HCl does the lion's share of the work of reducing food into tiny bits that will more easily be dismantled by enzymes in the small intestines. Your meal won't pass from your stomach into your intestines until it's reached the proper acidic pH; when HCl levels are low, this process takes considerably longer, so long, in fact, that sometimes the stomach will begin to send bits of food mixed with acids and enzymes back up the esophagus, causing a burning sensation you know as heartburn. Insufficient HCl production can also predispose you to gas, bloating, flatulence, constipation, or diarrhea.

The acids found in apple cider vinegar can fill in if your HCl production is lacking. The enzymes and healthy bacteria in apple cider vinegar encourage healthy function of the digestive system. Sipping an apple cider vinegar tonic in room-temperature water before each meal will help prepare your stomach for the digestive process and get your digestive juices brewing, and it will add a little bit of extra acidity to make things run more smoothly.

Dizziness

Some say that dizziness can be relieved by drinking a glass of water containing a healthy splash of apple cider vinegar . . . I wouldn't let it go to your head!

Ear Infections

A study from Ohio State University has shown that irrigating (rinsing) infected ears with vinegar solution helps patients get well faster. You can use a vinegar rinse for ear infections or swimmer's ear. Use one-third rubbing alcohol, one-third vinegar, and one-third distilled water. Squirt some into the ear canal with an ear syringe, let it sit for a minute or so, then turn your head and let it drain out. Repeat on the other side. Do this once a day until symptoms subside. This treatment also works for your pets!

Eye Health

Remember your mom telling you that eating carrots would improve your vision? She was right—beta-carotene in carrots supports eye health in two ways. First, it can be made into vitamin A, from which some eye tissues are built; one of the symptoms of severe vitamin A deficiency in children is a blinding eye disease called xerophthalmia. Second, beta-carotene from carrots (and apple cider vinegar) contributes to eye health by protecting against cataracts. Oxidation—the attack of free radicals—on the eye's lens can lead to the cloudiness and loss of color vision typical of cataracts and beta-carotene helps to neutralize those free radicals before they do their damage.

Fatigue

Buildup of lactic acid in the body, which may occur during exercise or stress, can be a cause of fatigue. Amino acids found in apple cider vinegar can counteract the effects of excess lactic acid in the bloodstream. Potassium and enzymes in vinegar may also play a part in treating fatigue.

Food Poisoning

The antiseptic and disinfectant qualities of vinegar are useful preventatives against the ill effects of eating spoiled food. Vinegar neutralizes poisons and kills harmful bacteria in the digestive tract. If you're eating

Samurai Rice Vinegar Tonic for Strength and Power

In ancient Japan, samurai warriors made a special tonic that was said to give them strength and power. *Tamago-su* was made by immersing a whole raw egg in a cup of rice vinegar and allowing it to sit undisturbed for a week. At the end of the week's time, the vinegar would dissolve all but the membrane that separates the shell from the white and yolk. This membrane was broken and the contents were dumped back into the vinegar. After throwing the membrane away, the warrior would mix the tonic thoroughly and take a small amount three times daily, stirred into a glass of hot water. It is still said that this practice ensures a long and healthy life.

questionable food or food that's being served to you in another country, you would do well to take 1 to 2 tablespoons of vinegar in some water before your meal. If food poisoning symptoms begin to arise after a meal, take a ¼ teaspoon of apple cider vinegar, straight up.

Make sure you eat your rice and pickled ginger when you go out for sushi. Parasites can take up residence in raw fish, and they can make you sick when they take up residence in your digestive tract. Sushi rice is mixed with parasite-stopping rice vinegar and the ginger is pickled in the same tart, sweet liquid. Ginger itself has some powerful antiparasite action, as does that spicy green sushi accompaniment known as *wasabi*.

Gallstones and Kidney Stones

Vinegar is a beneficial preventive and curative for kidney stones and gallstones. If stones grow too large to be eliminated naturally, medical treatments may become necessary to break them up so that they can leave the body. Anyone who's had a kidney stone will tell you that the pain is among the worst a person can experience.

These stones are made of hardened calcium deposits, and it's thought that malic acid, enzymes, and pectins in vinegar work as solvents to soften or dissolve the stones. Gallstones and kidney stones are relatively unknown problems in areas or households where vinegar is frequently used.

Naturopath Patricia Bragg recommends a treatment called a *gallbladder flush*. Fill an 8-ounce glass with one part virgin olive oil, two parts organic apple juice, and a teaspoon of apple cider vinegar. Drink it down, and repeat twice more on the first day. Sleep on your right side, pulling your right knee toward your chest; this opens the way for stones to pass. On the second day of the flush, only take the mixture twice. During the gallbladder flush, eat no solid food; drink only organic apple juice for both days. On the third day, eat a raw salad with a dressing made from apple cider vinegar and olive oil (see recipe in "Vinegar Cooking Tips" on page 92). Hopefully you'll see tiny, greenish-brown stones in your bowel movements after doing this flush.

An alternate method for the gallbladder flush is to eat nothing but apples all day long and to drink a cup of olive oil right before bed.

Headache

Headaches are messengers from your body that tell you something is amiss and needs attention. Subtle imbalances in your liver, gallbladder, kidneys, or other organs could trigger headache pain; so could allergies, fatigue, or emotional stress. While vinegar isn't a cure-all for headaches, it can be an effective remedy for some.

Research has shown that urine becomes more alkaline than normal when headaches strike—an indication that the body is somewhat out of balance. Here, the acids in apple cider vinegar may help by assisting the kidneys to restore proper acid/alkaline balance.

Inhaling vaporized apple cider vinegar may provide relief for some headache sufferers. In a pan, boil a splash or two of apple cider vinegar with some water. As steam begins to rise, remove it from the heat source. Place the pan on a counter or table and toss a towel over your head as you lean over the pan, breathing in the vapors from the steaming vinegar-water mixture. (Don't breathe in too deeply and burn yourself! Test the steam gently first.)

If you own an electric vaporizer, add some apple cider vinegar to the water and breathe the vapors for five minutes.

Heatstroke

Apple cider vinegar tonic makes a great restorative on hot days. It's rich in minerals and electrolytes lost through sweat. It can work to lower the high blood pressure typical of heatstroke. In the olden days, a drink called "switchel" was served to fortify exhausted farm workers: 2 tablespoons of apple cider vinegar, 1½ tablespoons of blackstrap molasses, and 2 cups boiling water were combined and poured over ice. Blackstrap molasses is an excellent source of magnesium and iron.

Hiccups

If you *slowly* sip a glass of warm water with 1 teaspoon of vinegar mixed in, hiccups will usually stop. This treatment works even better when you sip from the far side of the glass.

Indigestion

Contrary to popular belief, indigestion (and heartburn) are most often not due to *excess* stomach acid; usually, a lack of or underproduction of stomach acid is to blame.

Normally, your stomach digests food with strong hydrochloric acid (HCl) and pepsin, an enzyme active only in an acid environment. When underacidity is remedied by taking apple cider vinegar before a meal, the flow of nutrients to the body is improved—and you feel more energetic and healthy.

The malic and tartaric acids contained in apple cider vinegar improve digestion by restoring proper acidity, and also by inhibiting the growth of unfriendly bacteria in the digestive tract.

Some natural health practitioners believe that liver stagnation is a cause of indigestion. Apple cider vinegar has long been regarded as a highly activating and detoxifying natural medicine that counteracts the effects of rich, greasy foods. It functions as a solvent to break down fats and protein and dissolve minerals for improved assimilation.

To soothe indigestion, take 1 tablespoon of vinegar in half a glass of water after a heavy meal. Taken just before a meal, this tonic can prevent indigestion altogether. It stimulates the flow of saliva and other digestive juices.

Morning Sickness

Almost half of all pregnant women experience nausea and vomiting during the first three months of pregnancy. In some, these symptoms last far past the morning hours and into the second and even third trimesters of pregnancy, making it difficult for the mother to get enough nourishment to fuel her own body and the body of her growing baby. Drinking a glass of room-temperature water with a teaspoon of apple cider vinegar can help to keep morning sickness at bay.

Women often become anemic due to iron deficiency during the first three months of pregnancy. The "switchel" tonic with apple cider vinegar, blackstrap molasses, and water described earlier could supply needed iron.

Muscle Soreness

Sore muscles may be the result of excess lactic acid accumulation in muscle tissues. A dose of vinegar in water works in the body to precipitate accumulated acid crystals, placing them in solution so that they can be flushed out of the body through the organs of elimination. The dosage called for in cases of muscle soreness is: 1 or 2 teaspoons of apple cider vinegar in a glass of water. A spoonful or two of raw honey may be added.

Stiffness in and around the joints may also be due to a potassium deficiency. As I noted earlier, potassium is plentiful in apple cider vinegar, and this mineral boost can help further relieve muscle soreness and aching joints.

To soothe tired or sprained muscles, try wrapping the afflicted area with a cloth dipped in apple cider vinegar and wrung out. Leave the cloth on for five minutes, and you just might feel your vim and vigor returning! Add a dash of cayenne pepper for extra warmth.

Stiff neck? Try an apple cider vinegar poultice. Soak a rag in one part each of vinegar and warm water. Wring it out and wrap it around your neck, then cover it with plastic wrap and a towel. If you're dealing with bruised or swollen areas, use cold water instead of hot. For allover aches and pains, soak in a tub of warm water into which you've poured 2 to 3 cups of apple cider vinegar.

Nasal Congestion/Sinuses

Many suffer the discomfort of excess mucus in the nose, throat, or sinus cavities. Often, this mucus can cause obstructions that lead to painful sinus infections. A daily vinegar tonic can cut down on mucus drainage. For more serious nasal or sinus mucus problems, make a mixture of warm water and 1 to 2 tablespoons of apple cider vinegar. Hold a small amount cupped in the palm of your hand, plug one nostril, place the other nostril into the vinegar mixture, and sniff hard. You'll get the disinfecting and mucus-cutting power of apple cider vinegar deep into your sinus cavities. Allow it to run down the back of your throat; spit it out through your mouth if you would rather not swallow it. Then, repeat with the other nostril, and repeat again on both sides.

Sore Throat

Sore throat can be caused by either viruses or bacteria. If you develop a sore throat, try this apple cider vinegar cocktail: Mix ¼ cup honey and ¼ cup apple cider vinegar and take a tablespoon of the mixture every four hours, or more often if you feel you need to do so. Or, try ½ cup apple cider vinegar mixed with ½ cup water, a teaspoon of cayenne pepper, and 3 tablespoons of honey; take this on the same sort of schedule, every four hours or so.

At the first sign of a sore throat, send in germ-fighting apple cider vinegar in the form of a gargle. Mix one part vinegar and one part warm water and gargle every hour until symptoms are relieved. Gargling with apple cider vinegar will help cut mucus and freshen your breath, too! Be sure to rinse the mouth—but not the throat—with fresh water to prevent the erosion of tooth enamel by acids in the vinegar.

If you're susceptible to sore throats or laryngitis, it's a good idea to gargle apple cider vinegar solution once or twice a week to ward off germs in the throat.

Ulcers

A controlled study published in the *Japanese Journal of Pharmacology* indicates that vinegar may prompt the stomach lining to mount a natural defense against ulcers induced by overconsumption of alcohol. Additional research proving that vinegar can prevent stomach ulcers due to other causes has yet to be conducted; however, since this early study showed that vinegar offered over 95 percent protection against alcohol-induced ulcers, the possibility that vinegar may someday be used to prevent other types of ulcers looks promising.

Urinary Tract Infection

Maintaining the proper acidity of the urinary tract creates an inhospitable environment for bacteria and yeasts that can cause painful infections. Sipping an apple cider vinegar tonic daily can help you to keep the right pH balance in the urinary tract, kidneys, bladder, and vagina.

Cranberry juice is a well-known natural remedy for urinary tract infections. It prevents bacteria from attaching to the walls of the urinary passage. To harness the healing power of both cranberries *and* apple cider vinegar, add some cranberry juice to your apple cider vinegar tonic and sweeten it with a tablespoon of honey or some organic grape juice.

Yeast Infection

Yeast infections, also known as *candidiasis,* are caused by a yeast called *candida albicans.* Candida yeasts naturally exist in the body, striking a harmonious balance with other organisms that live there, including "good"probiotic bacteria. When the pH of the vagina is altered, probiotic bacteria can't thrive and yeasts flourish, quickly overgrowing. A vinegar-and-water douche effectively changes vaginal pH, nipping yeast growth in the bud. The vinegar will also kill off other infectious bacteria. Douche twice a day with a solution of half vinegar (white vinegar works well) and half room-temperature water until symptoms disappear.

Don't use vinegar douches on a regular basis, because recent research has shown that too-frequent douching can cause more harm than good. Because yeast infections tend to recur, it's important to learn what sets the condition off in your body and to make adjustments accordingly. The pH balance and probiotic populations of the vagina can be disturbed by antibiotic use or a diet too high in simple sugars.

Vaginal infections may also be caused by a bacterium called *trichomonas.* Such infections can cause an unpleasant discharge and fishy odor. Conventional doctors like to prescribe a strong antibiotic for this problem, but for pregnant women, vinegar douching is prescribed instead. It works even if you're not pregnant!

A vinegar bath can also improve symptoms of vaginal or urinary tract infections: add a cup of apple cider vinegar to a warm sitz bath twice daily.

HERBAL VINEGAR PRESCRIPTIONS

When you combine the healing power of vinegar with the medicinal qualities of herbs, you've got a winning combination. For directions on how to make infused vinegars, look back to page 22.

Acacia Vinegar

Dabbing this herbal vinegar onto the gum area around an aching tooth is said to help relieve toothache pain.

Clove Vinegar

Used in ancient China as an aphrodisiac, clove vinegar is also a good remedy for vomiting.

Dandelion Vinegar

Vinegar infused with dandelion leaves has laxative and liver-cleansing effects. It also acts as a mild diuretic, flushing away excess fluid and possibly lowering blood pressure that has crept too high. It's also said that dandelion vinegar is healing for intestinal inflammations. If you suffer from irritable bowel syndrome or colitis, 1 or 2 tablespoons of dandelion vinegar in water could be just what the doctor ordered.

Garlic Vinegar

Garlic is a healing herb with a long history of use for a variety of ailments. It has antibiotic, antiviral, antifungal, anticancer, and heart-protective effects. Use garlic vinegar often in cooking and dressings.

Myrrh Vinegar

Swish a tonic made with this herbal vinegar (1 to 2 tablespoons in a cup of water) in your mouth to heal inflamed gums and freshen your breath. Remember to rinse afterward with water.

Peppermint Vinegar

Mint is a calming remedy for a gassy, upset, or crampy digestive system. Mix 1 to 3 tablespoons of peppermint-infused vinegar, a teapoon of honey, and water, and sip for a delicious digestive remedy. Spearmint will have similar effects when made into a vinegar infusion.

Rosemary Vinegar

Shakespeare's Hamlet said that rosemary is for remembrance; ancient Greek students twined rosemary sprigs into their hair to improve their brain function. Using rosemary vinegar for cooking and in salad dressings will fortify your memory and help to cure dizziness and tension headaches. Rosemary also contains potent antioxidant substances that have been shown to slow the growth of cancer cells.

Eucalyptus Vinegar

Traditionally, eucalyptus oil has been used to open up breathing passages constricted by colds or asthma. Try an infusion of eucalyptus in some apple cider vinegar when you use a vaporizer or boiled vinegar water to open up breathing tubes (see page 54 for a review of this treatment). The warming power of eucalyptus vinegar can also be used in the vinegar salve for arthritic joints on page 41. *Don't take this vinegar internally.*

Lavender Vinegar

Use the soothing scent of lavender to calm an overwrought nervous system. Add a cup or two of lavender-scented apple cider vinegar to your bath water for sweet-smelling, soft skin and a more serene outlook.

Thyme Vinegar

Vinegar infused with thyme makes a delicious tenderizing marinade for meats. Smooth it onto fungal skin infections to speed healing.

Wormwood Vinegar

Don't take this bitter, pungent mixture internally. Use it on skin to deter fleas and other insects. You can also sprinkle it on your carpet to rid your home of infestations. Wormwood vinegar can also be used to treat wounds.

EXTERNAL BENEFITS OF VINEGAR

Now that you've heard the "inside story" on vinegar, let's turn our attention to the external medicinal values of vinegar.

Acne Blemishes

For acne blemishes, mix 2 tablespoons of apple cider vinegar with a cup of water and keep it in your bathroom. Several times a day, dab some of this mixture onto blemishes to help curb infection and dry out inflammation.

Athlete's Foot

Both athlete's foot and toenail fungus are fungal infections. They are notoriously difficult to get rid of, and mainstream medicine has yet to come up with a cure that works for everyone. Believe it or not, simple vinegar is one of the best treatments around. When you make the pH of the feet or nails more acidic, fungus is no longer able to grow well in that area.

For athlete's foot, soak a pair of socks in vinegar water—one part vinegar to five parts water—and wear for thirty minutes. You can use either apple cider vinegar or plain white vinegar. Or, if you're not faint at heart, you can soak your feet in straight vinegar for a few minutes a day until symptoms clear. For toenail fungus, use a dropper to apply vinegar directly to affected nails. Repeat daily until the nails appear normal again.

Bleeding

Vinegar helps blood to clot and congeal, speeding the rate at which bleeding stops. When a cut is swabbed with vinegar, it is less likely to become infected. People who use vinegar regularly heal faster from cuts and abrasions.

For nosebleeds, soak a cotton ball in apple cider vinegar and insert it into the nostril or nostrils. Tilt your head back slightly and pinch your nose closed for up to five minutes. Remove the cotton; if your nose is still bleeding, repeat the procedure.

Burns

Vinegar feels cool and soothing when applied to burns, whether they're from too much sunshine or from contact with a hot surface. The pH of apple cider vinegar matches that of human skin. Dab apple cider vinegar directly onto burns to ease discomfort, stave off infection, and supply nutrients necessary for healing.

While it's important for you to get some direct exposure to the sun so that your body can produce bone-building vitamin D, you should not stay out in it long enough to get burned. If you avoid sunburn, you're also less likely to develop age spots and deep wrinkles as you age. Some people swear by red wine vinegar, sprayed onto the skin, to help speed tanning and decrease burning when they spend time in the sun. A mixture of half olive oil and half apple cider vinegar, smoothed onto the skin, can also prevent sunburn and windburn.

A vinegar bath is soothing to sunburned skin. Fill a bathtub with lukewarm water, add a cup of apple cider vinegar, climb in, and relax! Or, gently sponge sunburned areas with straight apple cider vinegar.

Corn and Callus Treatment

A vinegar compress can get rid of unsightly corns or calluses overnight. Soak a half-slice of stale bread in apple cider vinegar, and securely tape it to the part of the foot you wish to treat. (If you want to avoid leaving crumbs in your bed, slip a cotton sock over the foot as well.) By morning, the skin should look smooth and new!

You can also try soaking your feet in a shallow pan of warm water that contains a cup of apple cider vinegar. Soak for half an hour, then rub calluses and corns down with a clean pumice stone.

Foot Odor

Soaking feet in a pan of warm water with ⅓ cup of vinegar two to three times weekly should get rid of foot odor. Foot odor is caused by bacteria, and the vinegar soak creates an inhospitable environment for those bacteria.

Hair and Scalp

Itchy scalp and dandruff are often caused by bacteria that clog hair follicles, forming dry crusts that itch and flake. The acids and enzymes in apple cider vinegar kill the offending bacteria. Some dandruff is caused by fungus, and apple cider vinegar will kill that, too! Simply pour full-strength vinegar on your head and work it into the roots of the hair, then wrap your head with a towel; let the treatment work for a full hour before washing your hair. Repeat the procedure as many times as necessary to do away with dandruff and itchy scalp for good.

Hemorrhoids

The painful swelling of hemorrhoids can be relieved by dabbing some undiluted apple cider vinegar directly on the inflammation with a cotton ball. If the vinegar burns, dilute it half-and-half with water before applying again. Reapply every few hours until symptoms are relieved. Topical vinegar also helps to soothe rectal itching.

Herpes

To relieve the discomfort of both cold sores and genital herpes sores—both caused by herpes viruses—apply apple cider vinegar to affected areas of skin. Itching and burning will quickly dissipate once the vinegar is applied; vinegar will also speed healing.

Shingles sores, which are caused by the herpes zoster virus, can also be soothed and healing promoted with the application of undiluted apple cider vinegar.

Impetigo

This bacterial infection of the skin can strike people of any age, but it seems to be especially prevalent in children. It's very contagious and can pass like wildfire around groups of kids who play or attend school together. Impetigo causes blisters that erupt and peel away; it's not terribly painful, but looks unsightly and can be hard to get rid of without antibiotics—unless you know how to use vinegar to cure the problem!

Swab apple cider vinegar onto impetigo lesions at least three times daily. After five days have passed, if the impetigo has not disappeared, try swabbing the skin more often.

Insect Bites and Stings

Itchy bites, stings, welts, hives, or swellings can be soothed with a paste of cornstarch moistened with vinegar. This mixture will help to draw fluid out of the itchy area, decreasing inflammation and the uncomfortable sensations that often accompany it. You can also pat undiluted apple cider vinegar directly onto itchy areas to quickly cool and relieve discomfort.

It's said that a daily vinegar tonic works to repel mosquitoes, too!

Jellyfish Stings

Next time you take your family to the beach, make sure you stow a little bottle of vinegar in your beach bag next to your sunscreen, towels, and summer reading. According to the Massachusetts College of Pharmacy and Allied Health Sciences, vinegar is your best remedy against the painful and potentially dangerous sting of a jellyfish.

As soon as you feel the burning sensation of a jellyfish sting, splash vinegar over the area. It will quickly soothe the pain. Keep vinegar on the area in the form of a soak or compress. Vinegar reacts with the skin to neutralize the poison that causes the painful reaction, and so should lessen the severity of the sting. This remedy also works for stings and bites from other creatures that live on land and in the water.

Poison Ivy and Poison Oak

A mixture of equal parts apple cider vinegar and water or apple cider vinegar and rubbing alcohol relieves the itching caused by poison ivy, poison oak, or nettle stings. Just dab the mixture onto the affected area.

Or, put equal parts distilled water and apple cider vinegar into a spray bottle and chill in the refrigerator or freezer until very cold, then spray onto rashes. The cold will compound the soothing relief the apple cider vinegar provides.

Ringworm

The characteristic reddish, raised, half-circular rash caused by ringworm *(Tinea corporis)* can be hard to get rid of and is very contagious. Children can catch this fungal infection from each other or from family pets. It can strike on the skin of the scalp or elsewhere on the body, and can cause uncomfortable inflammation and itching.

Apply the antiseptic power of apple cider vinegar, undiluted, to affected areas six times daily. Use your fingers, a cottonball, or a gauze square.

Thrush

When yeasts become overgrown in the mouth or on the nipples of nursing mothers, the diagnosis is thrush. The same *candida* yeast causes both thrush and vaginal yeast infections. Thrush in the mouth is a common side effect of antibiotic and oral or inhaled steroid use.

You can use a vinegar solution to fix the problem. Mix 4 tablespoons of apple cider vinegar in a gallon of water. Drink an entire gallon of this vinegar tonic per day. You can also try rinsing your mouth with diluted apple cider vinegar. If you're a nursing mother with a painful thrush infection on your nipples, swab undiluted apple cider vinegar directly onto your nipples and let them air-dry. Wipe the vinegar residue off before nursing your baby again. This can help relieve symptoms as well as remedy the underlying problem of yeast overgrowth.

Weight Control

According to folk medicine, a single teaspoon of apple cider vinegar in a glass of warm water before each meal will melt away excess pounds. No one is sure how this regimen might work; it may be because (a) it really does pump your metabolism up a notch to burn more calories; (b) its fiber, mixed with the water, helps to take the edge off the appetite by filling the stomach a bit before the start of a meal; or (c) the potassium in apple cider vinegar helps to flush away retained fluids. No matter—the effect is the same. If it works for you, you needn't understand why!

Apple cider vinegar is also beneficial for underweight conditions. This may be due to its ability to help the body digest, assimilate, and utilize nutrients more efficiently and thoroughly.

BODY BEAUTIFUL

The miracles of vinegar don't cease with the internal and external medicinal uses I've described so far. Vinegar is also a valuable cosmetic aid that can help you look better from head to toe—and when you look better, you feel better!

After-Shower Rinse

Rub your body down with a mixture of half apple cider vinegar and half water. This will rinse soap scum and mineral deposits from your skin, leaving it soft and smooth. You needn't rinse after applying this invigorating rubdown!

Cut and Abrasion Treatment

Swab cuts and abrasions with full-strength vinegar to kill bacteria and prevent infection.

Deep-Clean Skin

Deep-clean your skin with ingredients from all over the kitchen. You'll need:

1   egg yolk
1   teaspoon apple cider vinegar
1   teaspoon lemon juice
¼   cup olive oil
1   teaspoon baking soda

Thoroughly mix egg, vinegar, lemon juice, and oil. Add the baking soda and stir. Apply and massage well into skin with fingertips. Rinse with warm water and pat dry.

Facial Treatments

To prevent or eliminate facial blemishes and acne, try an apple cider vinegar facial. First, steam-clean your face over a pot of steaming vinegar water. Pour a cup of apple cider vinegar into a quart of water and heat it in a pot on your stove. Once it begins to boil, remove it from the heat and lean over it with a towel draped over your head.

This will open your pores in preparation for the next step of your vinegar beauty treatment.

Next, dampen a cotton ball with undiluted vinegar and gently wipe it over your face. If you have blemishes, you can dab aloe vera gel on to speed healing and reduce the chance of scarring. It's easy to grow a little aloe plant in a pot; that way, you can always break off a leaf for some fresh aloe gel. Finally, spray your face with a chilled mixture of half apple cider vinegar and half distilled water to tone and close pores. Isn't that refreshing?

Here's a facial that is good for people with oily skin. Wash your face with just warm water, then open pores with a washcloth soaked in hot water and wrung out; leave it on for three minutes. Soak another, thinner cloth in apple cider vinegar water (2 tablespoons apple cider vinegar to each cup of water) and place over your face, with a hot-water–soaked and wrung-out washcloth over it. Lie with your feet elevated on a couch or wall to move circulating blood toward the head and face. Remain there for at least ten minutes, then

---

Bee Aware of Honey!

Honey is food collected and predigested by bees. The nectar from thousands of flowers is processed into a thick, luscious liquid composed mostly of simple sugars: dextrose (pure glucose) and levulose. In addition, honey is packed with amino acids, trace elements, enzymes, protein, phosphorus, carbohydrates, calcium, niacin, potassium, and iron. It's a golden, delicious, liquid multivitamin. And honey requires no refrigeration; it is naturally antiseptic and will not support the growth of mold or bacteria.

Sour vinegar and sweet honey. Who says opposites don't attract?

remove the cloths and rub your facial skin gently upward with a towel or loofah. This will remove dead, dry skin. Repeat this facial once weekly for best results.

If you're prone to blackheads and pimples, try a nourishing strawberry vinegar facial. Mash three large strawberries into ¼ cup vinegar and allow to steep for two hours. Strain the mixture through a cloth, then pat the deep pink strawberry vinegar onto your face and neck before going to bed. Leave it on until you rise the next morning.

Fingernail Smoother

I'd rather you didn't use nail polish on a regular basis. It contains potent chemical toxins that can be breathed into your lungs and can soak into your skin. Of course, I understand that some special occasions merit the use of nail polish, and some professions require nails to be neatly manicured. Always apply nail polish in a well-ventilated area, and minimize its contact with your skin.

The Importance of Healthy Skin

The health of your skin mirrors the health of your body. The skin is your largest organ, weighing an average of 15 percent of your total body weight and covering an average of 6 square feet. Your skin protects your internal tissues against harm; helps to control body temperature; responds to environmental stimuli; sweats out water, salts, and toxic compounds; and synthesizes vitamin D.

Your skin requires a constant supply of many nutrients because it is composed of rapidly dividing cells, which are sensitive to nutrient status. Vinegar is nutrient rich, and its pH is nearly identical to that of healthy skin. Smooth some onto your face or arms and you'll see how soothing and cooling it can be!

Cleaning your fingernails with white vinegar before applying polish will allow for a smoother, longer-lasting manicure.

Hand Wash

Heavily soiled hands can be effectively cleaned with cornmeal moistened with apple cider vinegar. Scrub, rinse, and pat dry.

Healthy Hair

Apple cider vinegar has long been used to brighten hair. According to one folk remedy, drinking a mixture of water, 4 teaspoons of apple cider vinegar, 4 teaspoons of honey, and 4 teaspoons of blackstrap molasses causes hair to shine with rich color.

Rinse after each shampoo with ½ cup of apple cider vinegar mixed with 2 cups of warm water. This rinse will brighten dark hair, add sparkle to blonde hair, and remove buildup that can result from using styling products and inexpensive shampoos.

If you're the victim of an overly frizzy permanent, you'll be glad to know that this vinegar rinse will calm the frizz quite nicely. A vinegar rinse will also kill a pesky microorganism called *bottle bacillus*, which is a common cause of scalp conditions such as dandruff.

Itchy Skin

Soap can cause an itchy alkaline reaction in some people. Substitute a solution of half apple cider vinegar and half water for soap. Rub your body down with this solution while bathing, as you would with soap. It will leave your skin feeling naturally soft with a normalized pH balance, and totally free of soap scum.

Lice

To help get rid of lice and eggs without applying harmful chemicals over and over again, try rubbing some apple cider vinegar into the roots of the hair and dipping the nit comb into apple cider vinegar.

Liver Spots

These darkened brownish areas of skin, sometimes called age spots, can be lightened with this vinegar treatment. Wipe the area daily with a teaspoon of onion juice and two teaspoons of vinegar. You can accomplish the same end by cutting an onion in half and dipping it into some vinegar before rubbing it on age-spotted areas of the skin. According to those who have used this folk remedy, you'll see the spots beginning to fade within a few weeks.

Underarm Deodorizer

The natural odor of a healthy body shouldn't be offensive; if you eat right and keep yourself clean, you may not even need chemical deodorants or antiperspirants to prevent body odor. You can use the power of apple cider vinegar to keep underarms free of odor-causing bacteria. Simply wipe some undiluted vinegar beneath your arms; don't rinse it away. Try it—it really works!

Varicose Veins

Susceptibility to varicose veins appears to be the luck of the draw. Some people never have a single one, while others have so many prominent veins that they feel uncomfortable about wearing shorts or short dresses. The tendency to develop varicose veins is mostly dictated by heredity.

Here's a time-tested folk remedy for varicose veins: Wrap the legs in a cloth dampened with undiluted apple cider vinegar. Elevate the legs and leave the cloth on for a half-hour. If you can keep this up each morning and night for six weeks, shrinking of varicose veins could be your reward! To accelerate the results of this treatment, follow each application of the vinegar compresses with a glass of warm water with 1 or 2 teaspoons of apple cider vinegar mixed in. Drink the tonic slowly.

PET HEALTH

It will probably come as no surprise when I tell you that vinegar is also good for what ails your beloved animal companions. Here are some of the ways you can put the healing power of vinegar to work for your furry friends.

Clean Up "Accidents"

If your pet urinates on the carpet or furniture, sprinkle vinegar onto the soiled area. After the vinegar has had a few minutes to loosen stains and odors from carpet and fabric fibers, sponge it from the center of the stain outward. Finish by blotting with a dry cloth. You may need to repeat the process.

Daily Health Tonic

Some holistic vets recommend the daily use of apple cider vinegar for cats and dogs. It's good for their digestive tracts and helps to keep their coats shiny and healthy—and it's like giving your pet an all-natural vitamin and mineral supplement every day! Add a tablespoon of apple cider vinegar to your pet's water dish whenever you fill it.

Ear Care

Help your dog to stop scratching his ears by swabbing the insides of his ears with diluted vinegar.

To treat ear infections, make a mixture of one-third rubbing alcohol, one-third white vinegar, and one-third water. Use a dropper to put eight to ten drops in the animal's ear. Hold the animal's head sideways to allow the mixture to work, then drain. If the animal continues to scratch and rub his ears after three days of this treatment, take him to the veterinarian to be checked for mites or a serious bacterial infection.

Flea and Tick Deterrent

Add a teaspoon of vinegar to every quart of your pet's drinking water to deter fleas and ticks.

Horse Feed Supplement

Horses can develop intestinal stones called *enteroliths*. These stones can cause blockages that require expensive surgery and postsurgery care. Veterinary researchers at the University of California at Davis recommend 1 to 2 cups of apple cider vinegar daily to prevent enteroliths. Vinegar lowers intestinal pH in horses, which prevents stones from forming.

Pour ¼ cup of apple cider vinegar over your horse's grain. Flies will stay away, and your horse will love the taste!

Some horses respond to straight vinegar by developing diarrhea. If this happens to your horse, stop feeding the vinegar until stools become normal again, and try diluting the vinegar half-and-half with water next time.

Relief for Skin Conditions

Skin conditions can be a big problem for animals, especially dogs. If your pet suffers from itchy or painful skin eruptions, bathe him or her in a tub of warm water to which you've added a cup or two of apple cider vinegar.

Rinse Away the Smell of Skunk

If your pet has ever had a run-in with a skunk, you know firsthand that cleanup is an arduous and messy task. You can use vinegar instead of tomato juice. Your pet won't be too pleased to have a vinegar bath, but after it's all over you can shampoo your pet as you normally do to get rid of the vinegary smell.

Chapter Three

MIRACLES AROUND
HOME SWEET HOME

The Cleaning Power of Sour

Many commercial household cleaning products are harmful to the environment and to your wallet. Let's take a stroll through your house; I'll show you more safe, nontoxic ways to clean, deodorize, and disinfect with vinegar than you ever knew existed. You can clean practically everything in your home with vinegar—for pennies!

When using vinegar for cleaning, put away the good stuff and use inexpensive distilled white vinegar. It will cut grease and soap scum, inhibit mold, dissolve mineral buildup, and retard bacteria growth. Some people find the smell of vinegar unpleasant. If it bothers you, just add a squeeze of lemon to your vinegar cleaning solutions.

It's always a good idea to test vinegar cleansers on a small, inconspicuous part of carpets or furnishings before using them on large areas.

Ready to really clean up? Good. Let's start in the family room.

FAMILY ROOM

A spray bottle filled with full-strength white vinegar is your best bet for making dirty windows sparkle. Spray vinegar on and dry right away with a soft, clean cloth. For light maintenance cleaning, you can spray on a diluted formula of ¼ cup vinegar to a quart of water.

You can make an excellent solution for cleaning tile, linoleum, or wood floors with a cup of vinegar and a bucket of water. Pour the vinegar directly into your mop bucket, if you like. If you prefer to use another floor cleaner, use vinegar solution as a rinse to clear away residues that can dull the finish of your nice clean floor.

Remove light carpet stains by rubbing a vinegar-and-salt paste into the soiled area. Use 2 tablespoons of salt and ½ cup vinegar. Let the paste sit on the stain until it dries, then vacuum it up. For tougher carpet stains, add 2 tablespoons of borax to the paste before rubbing it into the carpet.

When pet accidents happen, pour undiluted vinegar directly on the stain and wipe clean with strong strokes. Then blot with cold water. The area is cleaned and sufficiently deodorized so the pet will not return to the "scene of the crime."

Furniture or woodwork that may have grown cloudy over the years can be brightened by rubbing with a solution of 1 tablespoon of clear vinegar in a quart of warm water. Buff to a luster using a soft, dry cloth.

If coaster-challenged guests have placed wet glasses on your furniture and left telltale white rings, they'll go away (the rings, not the guests) when you rub them with a mixture of equal parts white vinegar and olive oil.

To make your own furniture polish, mix ¼ cup linseed oil, ⅛ cup vinegar, and ⅛ cup whiskey. As the alcohol evaporates, so will the dirt! Or, try using three parts vinegar to one part lemon oil.

Iodine works to heal scratches on wood, too. Just a little iodine in equal parts with vinegar is all it takes. Apply with a small watercolor artist's paintbrush. More iodine deepens color and more vinegar will lighten color.

Wipe down vinyl surfaces with a combination of ½ cup each vinegar and water and 2 teaspoons of liquid soap. Rinse off with fresh water and buff dry.

Disinfect toys with a wee bit of vinegar and some hot water with a little soap. Rinse toys well after cleaning. If you're concerned about bacteria on toys that will go into children's mouths, use the disinfecting technique I describe at the end of page 84.

Leave the room smelling fresh by adding 1 teaspoon baking soda to 1 tablespoon of vinegar in 2 cups of water. After the foaming action subsides, pour this into a spray bottle, shake well, and spritz it into the air for a fresh fragrance. (Don't seal a foaming vinegar and baking soda solution until the foaming action has completely stopped; you'll end up with an explosion!)

Simmering a pot of water with about ¼ cup vinegar will also sweeten the air without adding a heavy "air-freshener" scent. You can add a dash of cinnamon, lavender, or other herbs to lend a noticeable scent to the room.

LAUNDRY ROOM

Now, let's step into the laundry room and over to the washing machine. Before you add your next load, pour in a full quart of vinegar and run a complete cycle. This will dissolve accumulated soap scum from the tub and the drain hoses for cleaner, trouble-free washing.

Hate the chemical smell that lingers in newly bought clothing? When washing new clothes for the first time, add a cup or two of white vinegar during the rinse cycle to help remove original manufacturing chemicals and their accompanying odor.

Add a ¼ cup of white vinegar to every load of wash to make colors and whites brighter. The vinegar also serves as a fabric softener and will inhibit germ growth, including athlete's foot germs on socks. A vinegar rinse will end static cling and even cut down on the lint clothes sometimes pick up during washing.

You can prevent bright colors from running in the washing machine by immersing the garment in undiluted white vinegar before washing. If you dye fabrics or clothing, do the same to set the dye before washing.

Perspiration odor and stains will disappear when clothes are pre-soaked overnight in 3 gallons of water mixed with ¼ cup vinegar.

You can rid your clothes of smoky tobacco odor by hanging them over a bathtub of hot water that has 2 cups of vinegar in it. (Full-strength vinegar will even absorb the odor of skunk on the skin!)

Remove grass, wine, berry, cola, coffee, or tea stains from washable fabrics by applying undiluted vinegar within twenty-four hours. Wash the fabric as usual.

If you use cloth diapers, you can feel good about protecting the environment, but you might find your indoor environment becomes pretty unpleasant from the odor of your diaper pail. To control odors and help remove stains, put a cup of distilled vinegar in 2 gallons of water into your diaper soak pail.

Ink stains on clothes can be removed by soaking in milk for one hour, then covering the stains with a paste of vinegar and cornstarch. When the paste dries, wash clothes as usual.

Some babies develop rashes due to irritating soap or uric acid residues in blankets, clothing, diapers, or sheets. Prevent this problem by adding a cup of vinegar to your rinse cycle. And why only baby the baby? The same procedure will reduce any alkalinity and soften the rest of the family's laundry as well!

If any body odor is emanating from that shirt or blouse you wanted to wear, sprinkle the armpits with vinegar and iron it: It will become fresh as a daisy!

And look at that iron. Any starch buildup making it stick? Wipe the sole plate when cold with full-strength white vinegar. Keep your iron free of mineral deposits by filling the water reservoir with straight white vinegar and steaming the iron clean with an old towel or rag. Repeat using water, then rinse the iron out thoroughly.

Light scorch marks on clothes may be removed by gently rubbing them with undiluted white vinegar, then wiping with a clean, white cloth.

Vinegar will also remove unsightly shiny patches from dark clothes. Just wipe the shiny area with undiluted white vinegar.

Hem marks left after altering hemlines or letting out seams may be gently rubbed with a cloth dampened in white vinegar, then steam-ironed. No telltale lines!

BATHROOM

And now, let's duck into the bathroom to see what other cleaning miracles we can achieve with our trusty bottle of distilled vinegar.

Wipe chrome and stainless steel fixtures with straight vinegar, then buff to a shine with a damp, soft cloth.

It's easy to keep plastic shower curtains free of ugly mold and mildew. Just put them through a short rinse cycle with a cup or two of vinegar. (Don't put plastic shower curtains in the dryer!) Maintain mold- and mildew-free shower curtains between washings by spraying them with a 50/50 mix of vinegar and water.

If you have sliding glass shower doors, built-up water scale is probably a fact of life in your bathroom. To clean water scale from glass, mix a teaspoon of aluminum sulfate (alum) with ¼ cup vinegar. Wipe the mixture onto the glass and scrub with a soft brush. Rinse thoroughly, then buff dry with a towel.

Wipe down ceramic or plastic surfaces with vinegar diluted with an equal amount of water. Because it can erode marble, avoid marble surfaces when cleaning with vinegar.

Clean stainless steel with baking soda that has been dampened with a small amount of vinegar.

To eliminate stains and odors in your toilet bowl, pour in a cup of undiluted white vinegar. Let it stand for about five to ten minutes, then flush away that unsightly ring.

For tougher toilet stains, pour vinegar on, then shake a little borax over the vinegar. Give it two hours to soak. Brush, then flush. The results will bowl you over!

Tackle tub and tile soap film with straight vinegar. Wipe surfaces, then rinse with water. For water scale buildup, mix ¼ cup vinegar with 1 teaspoon alum. Wipe the mixture on surfaces, then scrub with a small brush. Brush this solution on your shower head as well to dissolve mineral buildup that can cause clogs. Rinse with water and buff dry.

Clean combs and hairbrushes by soaking them for fifteen minutes in 2 cups of hot, soapy water mixed with ½ cup vinegar. Rinse clean in fresh water.

KITCHEN

That bottle of vinegar you have stored in the kitchen is there for cleaning, too. Eliminate streaks and bring out the shine on countertops and appliances by wiping them with a soft cloth well dampened with straight white vinegar. For extra gleam, wipe surfaces dry with a paper towel.

According to research scientist Susan Sumner from Virginia Polytechnic Institute and State University, vinegar and hydrogen peroxide are more effective at killing bacteria than chlorine bleach when used according to these guidelines: Fill one spray bottle with 3 percent hydrogen peroxide (the kind sold in drugstores) and another bottle with undiluted white or apple cider vinegar. Simply spray the surface you wish to disinfect with one, then the other, then wipe clean or rinse immediately;

that's all there is to it. It doesn't matter in what order you spray them, but don't make the mistake of mixing both into one bottle. The ingredients only work when sprayed on separately and wiped or rinsed off together. Dr. Sumner found that this treatment killed virtually all *salmonella, shigella,* and *e.coli* on heavily contaminated surfaces. Use this technique to disinfect cutting boards, countertops, even vegetables and fruit, or toys that go into babies' or small children's mouths.

The esteemed Yale–New Haven Hospital switched to vinegar cleaning solutions for the sinks in its surgery scrub room when the staff found that this actually worked better than the highly toxic commercial products they had been using.

When you have a lot of greasy mess to clean up, mix ¼ cup of vinegar with 2 cups hot water and stir in a teaspoon of borax. Pour the mixture in a spray bottle, spritz it on, then wipe grease away with a dry cloth. This is a good solution to use on exhaust fan grills.

Freshen your microwave by bringing a cup of water with ¼ cup vinegar in it to a boil on your microwave oven's highest setting. Set the temperature setting to "low" and boil for three minutes. After this, dry all interior surfaces and the back of the door. This leaves your microwave sparkling clean and deodorized.

Perk up the taste of your coffee by dissolving the lime and mineral deposits that are caked onto the heating elements of your electric coffee maker. Every so often, fill the reservoir with white vinegar and run it through the brew cycle. Do so twice if you haven't done a vinegar cleaning in some time. Afterward, rinse the coffeemaker by running through two cycles of plain water. Your coffee maker will then be ready to brew better-tasting coffee at a faster clip.

Remember how squeaky-clean vinegar gets your windows? The same goes for your glassware. Just add ½ cup vinegar to your dishwashing water to help eliminate water spotting. You can also put a cup of vinegar on the bottom rack of your automatic dishwasher for spotless results.

Stainless steel pots and pans turn out bright when scrubbed with a paste made from baking soda and vinegar. To get copper or brass cookware really clean, you'll need a more abrasive cleanser. Combine 2 teaspoons salt, 1 tablespoon flour, and just enough vinegar to form a paste. Scrub the metal with the paste, then rinse in water and polish with a dry cloth. For regular maintenance, wipe on a solution of equal parts vinegar and lemon juice with a paper towel and polish with a soft cloth. Believe it or not, you can also use ketchup—which contains vinegar—to do this job!

Here's another homemade metal cleaner for you to try: Mix 2 tablespoons cream of tartar with enough vinegar to form a paste. Rub the paste onto the metal and let it dry, then wash it off with warm water and dry with an old, soft towel.

Clean pewter with a paste of 1 tablespoon each of salt and flour with just enough vinegar to moisten. Wipe the paste over the pewter and allow it to dry. Then brush off the dried paste, rinse the pewter with hot water, and dry to a sparkling shine. An old-time variation on this technique for cleaning pewter uses cabbage leaves dampened in vinegar and dipped in salt. The cabbage leaves are then used to buff the pewter clean. Once this has been done, rinse and dry.

When you're stuck with stuck-on food, soak or simmer the cookware for a few minutes in 2 cups water and ½ cup vinegar. This will soften the hardened food and speed cleanup.

If you're using a sponge for kitchen cleanups, you can renew and disinfect it by soaking it overnight in a quart of hot water mixed with ¼ cup vinegar. Next day, the sponge will be clean, deodorized, and germ free.

It's a good idea to wipe down wood cutting boards at least once a week with full-strength white vinegar. You can also sprinkle and rub the wood with baking soda, then spray with vinegar, letting it sit for five minutes. The bubbling action cleans, deodorizes, and disinfects the boards. Rinse off in clear water.

Keep kitchen drains odor free and free flowing by pouring a handful of baking soda down the drain, followed by ½ cup white vinegar. Cover the drain for ten minutes, then run water down the drain. Whenever odor alone is the problem, just pour ½ cup distilled vinegar down the drain.

Clean and deodorize your garbage disposal by grinding up a tray of ice cubes made from undiluted vinegar. Flush the drain with cold water. Your disposal is now clean and fresh. A shortcut you can try: Pour regular ice cubes into the drain, then pour some vinegar over the ice cubes before grinding them up in the disposal.

Lunch boxes can be freshened overnight with a piece of bread soaked in vinegar.

Soak produce in a diluted vinegar solution for fifteen minutes to kill bacteria. Wash flesh foods with vinegar solution as well.

Lingering odors from smelly fish, cooked cabbage, or fresh-cut onions are nothing to cry about when you simmer a little vinegar in water in an uncovered pot. The offensive smell will be absorbed. Stale or smoky odors will also be absorbed by an open bowl of vinegar sitting out in the kitchen.

Problems with fruit flies in your kitchen? Put a bowl of apple cider vinegar outdoors, somewhere close to where they're hovering. The vinegar will draw them away from your kitchen. Roaches? Keep a spray bottle with undiluted distilled vinegar around, and use it to zap these pesky critters wherever they appear.

Clean brass and copper pots or decorative items by combining equal parts lemon juice and vinegar. Wipe this mixture on with a paper towel, then polish with a soft, dry cloth.

Rust spots on your pots and pans? Here's an old technique that really works: Fill the pot with hay or rhubarb. Add ¼ cup vinegar and enough water to cover the hay or rhubarb, then boil for one full hour. The rust will wipe easily away.

GARAGE

Now, let's step out into the garage. There's the car; let's go ahead and spritz all the chrome with vinegar and buff it to a gleaming shine.

And, hey, look at the windshield—there's a decal that expired three years ago. Soak it off with vinegar. While we're at it, let's use undiluted vinegar to dissolve that chewing gum on the floormat as well.

Whenever you have to leave your car outside in freezing weather, coat the windows with a mixture of three parts vinegar to one part water. This will keep windows frost free, and will save you the trouble of scraping ice off your windows in the morning when it's time to leave for work.

If any of your garage workshop projects require the removal of rusty blots or mineral accumulation, clean them up by soaking them in vinegar or applying full-strength vinegar to the affected areas. You can soak screws or nails in a sealed container overnight to remove rust.

Clean metal screens, storm doors, and aluminum lawn furniture with ¼ cup vinegar in a quart of water.

See those leather work shoes sitting in the corner, caked with salt or dirt? Clean them up by wiping them off with a cloth drenched with vinegar, then buff with a dry cloth. To preserve the leather, mix together 1 tablespoon each of vinegar and alcohol, 1 teaspoon of vegetable oil or beeswax, and ½ teaspoon liquid soap. Heat ingredients and when cool, work the mixture over the surface of the shoes. Buff them with a shoe brush until they gleam.

ARTS AND CRAFTS AREA

You can use vinegar where you do arts and crafts, too, whether it's your kitchen table, spare bedroom, backyard, or a special room you've set aside just for this purpose.

The next time you dye Easter eggs, add a teaspoon of vinegar and a teaspoon of food coloring to ½ cup boiling water. The colors will come out brighter.

There are those hardened paintbrushes you've been meaning to clean for months. Make the job easier by softening the old, dried paint with vinegar. Cover the bristles with boiling vinegar and let them stand for an hour, then rinse thoroughly. The next time you paint, keep in mind that a bowl of vinegar will absorb the odor of wet paint.

Do you work with wood? If so, you've likely had to clean up a wood glue spill. Glue of almost any kind can be softened for removal with undiluted vinegar. Wet down the excess glue with vinegar and keep it wet overnight; by morning it will come off easily.

Make a silvery, shiny wood stain with vinegar. Mix water-based ink into white vinegar and apply to wood with a soft, clean rag or brush.

To make fabric or leather glue, you'll need a sachet of clear gelatin, 3 tablespoons of white vinegar, 3 to 4 tablespoons of water, and 1 tablespoon of glycerin. Over low heat, melt the gelatin and the water, then add the rest of the ingredients. Mix well and apply while still warm. Pour what's left over into a small jar and heat to use again.

GREAT OUTDOORS

Come outside with me and I'll show you how you can use vinegar to tend your lawn and garden. Remember to clean your sunglasses with vinegar water before we go out into the sunshine.

When working with garden lime, splash your hands with undiluted vinegar to neutralize its roughening, drying effects. Be sure to rinse your hands with your garden hose after the vinegar wash.

Sandboxes can become litter boxes for pets and wild animals. To deter these opportunists, pour some vinegar into the sand every two months.

Keep cut flowers alive and blooming longer with vinegar. Into your vase, put 2 tablespoons of vinegar to a quart of warm water, then put in your cut flowers.

Improve seed germination in asparagus, okra, pea, and other woody-coated seeds by rubbing the seeds between two sheets of coarse sandpaper and soaking them overnight in a pint of warm water with ½ cup vinegar and a squirt of liquid soap. You can use this same soaking solution without the sandpaper step for nasturtium, parsley, turnip, or beet seeds.

To get rid of ants, spray a mixture of equal parts vinegar and water at possible points of entry—windowsills, door jambs, thresholds, and any foundation breaks. Ants will avoid the area, and you will have avoided using pesticides.

Chapter Four

MIRACLES ON THE MENU

Cooking with Vinegar

It seems natural to pair cranberry sauce with turkey, apple sauce with roast pork, a slice of lemon with fish, or mushrooms with steak. And it truly is natural to crave these accompaniments; our taste buds somehow know that cranberries, apples, lemons, and mushrooms contain natural acids which aid digestion. These acids help break down fats and protein and tenderize meat, and cause gastric juices and saliva to flow. (In case you were wondering, mushrooms are rich in citric acid.)

Vinegar's acid content is one of many reasons that Americans consume millions of gallons of this tart brew every year. Vinegar's acids tenderize vegetables such as cabbage, beets, carrots, and broccoli; they prevent enzymatic browning (darkening on exposure to air), which can produce an "off" flavor; they kill and inhibit the growth of bacteria (especially important with foods not intended for immediate consumption, such as deviled eggs or potato salad for picnics); and they make beans and other legumes more digestible and less gas producing.

Vinegar serves to balance the effect of salts you ingest and also dulls the craving for sweets. It contains only 2 calories per tablespoon and is free of fat and sodium.

You are probably taking in more vinegar than think. Vinegar is an ingredient in many condiments. Tomato ketchup alone accounts for 10 percent of the vinegar produced in America. You're also getting vinegar with every pickle you eat.

Vinegar clearly has a way to go before it is appreciated on a par with wines or even some cooking oils. A good chef or cook knows the importance of stocking a wide selection of high-quality vinegars, however, and knows that a vinegar that's just right for a particular salad or meat marinade would not do for other sauces or soups or for pickling purposes.

In most kitchens, vinegar is an indispensable ingredient with endless culinary uses. If you've never cooked with vinegar, you're in for a real treat as you learn how various vinegars deepen and expand the flavors of many foods. To demonstrate the versatility of vinegar, I've offered you recipes that span the menu, starting with a vinegar cocktail and ending with a vanilla yogurt, all containing that miraculous ingredient. Before I get into the recipes, however, I'd like to share with you some vinegar cooking tips that can save you a lot of time and effort in the kitchen.

VINEGAR COOKING TIPS

- Add 2 tablespoons of vinegar to boiling water when making hard-boiled eggs. The vinegar prevents the egg white from leaking out of any cracks during boiling and makes the shells peel off more easily. This also works with poached eggs, which will keep their shape better if vinegar is added to the poaching water.
- Add a teaspoon of white vinegar to rice boiling water to make rice fluffier and less sticky.
- If a recipe calls for buttermilk and you don't have any, add a tablespoon of vinegar to a cup of milk and let it stand for five minutes. Voila! A perfect substitute.
- To rescue a recipe that tastes either too sweet or too salty after ingredients are mixed, add a dash of vinegar to bring the flavors into balance.

- Wilted vegetables can be revived in a pan of ice water to which you've added a tablespoon of vinegar. This will also kill off any undesirable microorganisms.
- Try this simple vinegar salad dressing: Combine 1 tablespoon of apple cider vinegar, 1 teaspoon of olive oil, and one small dollop of clover honey.
- Splash some vinegar into dried beans during soaking and cooking to "predigest" them, which will make them less gas producing when eaten.
- Add a couple of dashes of rice vinegar to leftover rice to prevent spoilage and maintain good texture and taste.
- Adding some vinegar and salt to water used to soak produce will help to float pests out.
- Here's a marinade that decreases the formation of carcinogens in flame-broiled or grilled meats: Mix ½ cup packed brown sugar, 3 crushed garlic cloves, 1½ teaspoons salt, 3 tablespoons mustard, ¼ cup apple cider vinegar, 3 tablespoons lemon juice, and 6 tablespoons olive oil. Marinate overnight and brush onto meats during grilling.
- Rub vinegar on whole fish to make scaling easier and to prevent fishy-smelling hands.
- Ever buy a piece of ginger root, use a small amount, and watch the rest turn brown and shrivel up in your refrigerator? Use vinegar to preserve leftover ginger. Peel and grate the entire root and store in a jar of rice, sherry, or balsamic vinegar.
- To keep cheeses from hardening or growing moldy, wrap them in a cloth saturated with vinegar before sealing in an airtight container and refrigerating.
- Add a few drops of vinegar to pasta water to prevent sticking.
- How about a recipe for homemade cheese? You can use cow's milk or goat's milk for this recipe. Heat 3 gallons of fresh milk for forty-five minutes, stirring constantly. When the milk becomes hot and

foamy on top, cook for another fifteen minutes, then add ¼ cup vinegar and cook another fifteen minutes, continuing to stir slowly. Use a clean towel to strain out the whey, then stir ½ tablespoon salt into the curds. Place the curds in the center of a towel, then gather the edges of the towel above the cheese and wrap it snugly, fastening the top with a rubber band. Hang the wrapped cheese above a bowl so that the rest of the whey can drain out; this will take about an hour.

- If you're baking and you run out of eggs, you can substitute 1 tablespoon of white vinegar per needed egg.
- To replace baking powder, use ½ teaspoon apple cider vinegar and ¼ teaspoon baking soda for each teaspoon of baking powder called for in the recipe.

And now, let's have a nutrient-rich cocktail.

Rosy Red Vinegar Cocktail

1	quart tomato juice, chilled
1½	tablespoons red wine vinegar
1	white onion, grated
2	tablespoons honey
1	teaspoon garlic salt
2	tablespoons basil leaves, chopped
	Dash freshly ground black pepper

Combine all the ingredients in a large pitcher and mix thoroughly. Chill for at least one hour, allowing flavors to intermingle. Pour into short, frosty cold glasses and garnish with a wedge of lemon on the rim. Serves six.

It's refreshing, nonalcoholic, and highly nutritious! And it whets the appetite for the following appetizer.

Sweet and Sour Meatballs

1   small can pineapple, crushed (8 ounces)
½   cup apple cider vinegar
½   cup brown sugar, firmly packed
2   tablespoons soy sauce
½   teaspoon freshly grated ginger
1½   pounds organic, free-range ground beef
¾   cup cracker crumbs
¼   cup milk
1   egg, slightly beaten
1   teaspoon salt
     Dash freshly ground black pepper
1   tablespoon olive oil
1   tablespoon cornstarch
1   tablespoon water

Drain can of pineapple and set aside, saving juice. Add enough water to saved juice to make ¾ cup. Add vinegar, sugar, soy sauce, and ginger; set aside.

Mix meat with cracker crumbs, milk, egg, salt, and pepper. Form small meatballs using a rounded tablespoon for each. In a large frying pan, brown meatballs in oil. Add pineapple liquid, cover, and simmer for 15 minutes or until meatballs are done, stirring every 5 minutes. Stir in pineapple. Combine cornstarch and water, then pour into pan. Heat until the sauce thickens, stirring occasionally. This recipe will make enough for six people.

For the soup course, let's try the following healthy recipe.

Cold Gold Soup

1	medium cantaloupe
3	large peaches, ripe
½	cup orange juice, fresh squeezed
2	teaspoons honey
2	drops Tabasco sauce
	White pepper to taste
1	tablespoon balsamic vinegar
1	tablespoon mint, finely chopped
	Orange peel zest for garnish

Cut cantaloupe in half and scoop out seeds. Spoon flesh into a blender and puree. Peel peaches and cut into small chunks. Add to melon puree along with orange juice and honey. Blend until smooth. Stir in Tabasco and white pepper, cover, and chill at least one hour.

Stir in vinegar and chopped mint, then ladle soup into chilled bowls. Garnish with fresh whole mint leaves and orange peel zest. Serves six.

For our salad course, let's try a fresh bunch of mixed bitter greens with tomatoes and the following dressing.

Honolulu Lulu Dressing

6	tablespoons red wine vinegar
3	tablespoons water
2	tablespoons fresh lemon juice
2	tablespoons pineapple juice

¼   cup honey
½   teaspoon dry mustard
6   drops Tabasco sauce
¼   teaspoon celery seed
1   clove garlic, finely chopped
⅓   cup olive oil
     Freshly ground black pepper to taste

Stir together the first four liquid ingredients. Add honey, mustard, Tabasco, celery seed, and garlic. Whisk in the oil and fresh pepper. Cover and chill overnight for maximum "lulu" flavor. Yields about 1 cup.

For an entrée, may I suggest the following poached chicken and pasta salad.

Poached Chicken and Pasta Salad with Basil Vinaigrette

Basil Vinaigrette

2   egg yolks, room temperature
2   tablespoons Dijon mustard
1⅔   cups extra virgin olive oil
½   cup fresh basil leaves, chopped
¼   cup apple cider vinegar
⅓   cup warm water
      Freshly ground black pepper to taste

Blend egg yolks and mustard in a food processor. With the beaters turning, very slowly add the olive oil. Process until mixture emulsifies, then blend in the remaining ingredients.

Poached Chicken

> Cold water
> 1 tablespoon white wine
> Salt and pepper to taste
> 1 bay leaf
> Sprigs of fresh parsley and thyme
> 2 whole chicken breasts, boneless and skinless

Combine water, wine, salt, pepper, bay leaf, and sprigs of parsley and thyme in a large pot. Add chicken breasts, bring to a simmer, and cook until the breasts are tender. Remove from heat and allow meat to cool in the liquid. When cool, cut the breasts into thick strips.

Salad

> 1 pound salad-style pasta, cooked
> 1 cup snow peas
> 1 cup green beans
> 1 red bell pepper
> 1 cup cherry tomatoes
> ⅓ cup fresh basil, chopped
> 1 teaspoon thyme leaves
> Salt and pepper to taste

Steam peas and beans until slightly crunchy. Cut open pepper, remove seeds and membranes, and slice into strips. Halve the tomatoes.

Assembly: In a large bowl, combine pasta, chicken strips, bell pepper, tomatoes, basil, thyme, salt, and pepper. Pour dressing over all and toss lightly. Let stand one hour. Before serving, mix in snow peas and beans, and garnish with fresh basil. Serves six.

Let's have some sliced fruit or berries with Sweet Vanilla Yogurt for dessert.

Sweet Vanilla Yogurt

2   cups plain yogurt
4   teaspoons pure vanilla extract
6   tablespoons pure maple syrup
4   tablespoons peach, mango, or raspberry vinegar (if you don't
    have any of these, use apple cider or white wine vinegar)

Whisk all ingredients together in a stainless steel or glass bowl. Combine with a chilled fresh fruit salad or use as a dip for apple, peach, or pear slices, or for whole, ripe berries. Now *that's* a sweet treat that's good for you, too!

For after dinner, this raspberry vinegar cordial provides the finishing touch.

Raspberry Vinegar Cordial

In a glass bowl, combine 2 pounds of ripe raspberries and 1 pint of white wine or apple cider vinegar. Allow to steep at least 24 hours, then press out the juice from the berries. Strain the solution through cheesecloth and add 1 pound of granulated sugar.

Pour into a nonmetallic cooking pot and cook over moderate heat until the sugar dissolves. Bring to a boil and simmer until the mixture reaches the consistency of syrup. Makes about 4 cups.

To enjoy, sip straight or mix with water and ice in a tall glass.

Cherry Vinegar Cordial

Rinse 1 cup pitted cherries, then place them in a jar. Add
1 tablespoon sugar. Pour 1 pint of warm red wine or apple
cider vinegar over the cherries, seal the jar, and allow to stand
about 2 weeks before straining and bottling. Makes 1 pint.

Chapter Five

MAXIMIZING
YOUR HEALTH

My Comprehensive Plan

The body is self-healing and self-correcting when you give it a chance. Many degenerative diseases are affected by what you decide to eat and drink and how you choose to live. Many symptoms associated with advanced years are simply the end result of a lifetime of neglect, accompanied by natural nutritional deficiencies that can be forestalled—if not remedied—by making the right choices.

While it's true that heredity does create certain tendencies, *you are still in control of maximizing your health.* You can start feeling better in just days with a few targeted lifestyle and dietary changes.

Many believe that the need for multiple medicines and a general downturn in one's state of health are a natural part of growing older. Not so! Take me, for example. I'm pushing sixty and I'm not on high blood pressure medicine, heart drugs, or prostate medication. My weight is about where it should be, and my energy level is terrific.

In this chapter, I'm going to summarize my secrets for you. Over the past twenty-five years I've developed a simple yet comprehensive plan that anyone can gradually adopt at any time after deciding to maximize his or her health. Regardless of age or current condition, my plan will strengthen your overall health, prevent illness, and prolong your life.

EAT WHOLE FOODS

When you eat processed and refined foods, your body will shout, "I am what you eat." Your body doesn't need, nor does it know how to handle, commercially packaged foods that are devoid of natural nutrients but full of additives, dyes, sugar, salt, artificial sweeteners, and hydrogenated oils.

Switch to whole foods. Whole foods are those that come to your plate from gardens, orchards, free-range farms, and the sea, unadulterated and unprocessed. When you eat a variety of fresh vegetables, fruits, grains, beans, fish, meat, and poultry, you're getting healthy doses of the vitamins and minerals and other natural nutrients you need to combat symptoms of aging.

DRINK PURE, CLEAN WATER

Water is an overlooked essential nutrient. Stick to plain old H_2O; designer waters, coffee, tea, and soft drinks are not water substitutes. Good, clean water won't be found flowing from the tap, either, because most tap water is as processed as some packaged foods, and contains chlorine and other additives you don't need (and that can harm you). Get yourself a good home filtration system and drink six to ten glasses a day. You'll be amazed at how much better this small change will make you feel.

EAT MORE OF THE *RIGHT* FOODS

While meat and eggs aren't as bad for you as they've been made out to be by the medical mainstream, I recommend that you be choosy about the ones you eat. Free-range beef, wild game, eggs, and poultry are fine in moderation (that's one 3-ounce serving a day or less—about the size of a deck of cards). Think of these foods as condiments, or side dishes, that augment the flavors of plates full of fresh raw and cooked vegetables, beans, whole grains, and fresh fruit.

I'm a big fan of soy products. Soy foods such as tofu, tempeh, and miso give you plenty of protein, very little fat, a healthy dose of calcium (in the case of tofu made with calcium salts), and both soluble and insoluble fiber. Soy is nature's best source of genistein, a phytochemical that has weak estrogen-like effects in the body. Genistein has great promise as a preventive against cancers related to excessive amounts of stronger estrogens in the body. Soy foods may also strengthen bones and help women get through menopause more comfortably. Tofu is incredibly versatile—use soft versions in smoothies or sauces, and use firm versions to replace some or all of the meat in recipes from burgers to lasagna. Or, make a cup of delicious miso soup by dropping a rounded tablespoonful of this fermented soybean paste into a cup of water that has been brought to a boil and removed from the heat. Stir gently and add sliced scallions, cubed tofu, or even some rice noodles. Tempeh may be a little harder to get used to, but this food made from fermented soybeans can be used any time you might use meat.

Dairy products agree with some and not with others. If you wish to include dairy in your diet, make it organic and avoid products with added sugars. Organic plain yogurt is a winner—add your own fruit and some granola if you like. Organic cheeses have richer flavor than other types; grate a small amount over vegetables or use a thin slice to spice up a sandwich.

Cut way back on sugar! It's disguised in a lot of foods; sugar is added to everything from juices to breakfast cereals to condiments. Once you make a habit of indulging in sweet treats, it's difficult to kick the habit. Sugar has been implicated in most chronic diseases related to diet, including heart disease, diabetes, and arthritis. It's best also to avoid products made with refined flours, such as white bread, cakes, and cookies. Your body responds to refined flour much as it responds to pure sugar. It may seem impossible to eliminate or cut down on these foods—and I'm not saying it's easy—but once you've kicked your sugar and refined-flour habit, you'll be astonished at how much better you feel.

Try to eat some deepwater fish—salmon, cod, sardines, and albacore tuna are good choices—two to three times a week. These fish are rich in omega-3 oils, which have been shown to protect against a wide variety of problems, including heart disease and inflammatory conditions such as allergies and asthma. If you don't choose to eat fish, add omega-3s to your diet in the form of flaxseeds. Grind up a tablespoon of seeds in a coffee grinder and add to smoothies, cereals, or soups. (I'd rather you stay away from flaxseed oil, because it's so unstable that it is likely to be rancid by the time you get it home from the market. If the oil stays in the seeds, it's protected from oxidation.)

REDUCE OR AVOID RELIANCE ON DRUGS

I'm talking about *all* kinds of drugs. Prescription, over-the-counter, and so-called recreational drugs all incur side effects that can seriously harm you, even kill you. Even if you don't suffer serious harm, drugs can cause subtle side effects that adversely affect your quality of life.

Of course, modern medicine has made some miraculous strides, and drugs can be lifesaving if prudently used. The problem today is that drugs are relied on too heavily by conventional medical practitioners. Often, it's easier to hand a patient a prescription than to really seek out the cure for what ails him or her. When your doctor hands you a prescription, do your research and make sure it's something you really shouldn't do without. When you reach for the cold medicine or over-the-counter painkillers or antihistamines, stop a moment and consider whether you might benefit just as much from a nap, or a walk, or a day home from work, just resting.

To learn more about the risks you face when you use drugs, and to learn how to treat almost any health problem without them, refer to the book *Prescription Alternatives,* which I wrote with Virginia Hopkins.

GET A MOVE ON

Stop worrying about having to "work out." Instead, think only about adding more *movement* to your life. Doesn't that sound less intimidating and more like fun? You don't need to strain or sweat heavily to achieve the benefits of exercise: just move. Make any physical activity, from housework to yardwork to grocery shopping, into a time for moving your body. Even if you never get to the gym or run a marathon, you'll be improving your health simply by changing your attitude about what it means to get some exercise.

If at all possible, try to fit a brisk walk of thirty minutes into your day *at least* five days a week. Your stress level will decrease, your energy will increase, you'll sleep better, and you might even find that you look better!

ADOPT A SUPPLEMENTAL HEALTH PLAN

You need some insurance, but not the kind you get from a broker or agent. I'm talking about the health insurance that comes from reasonable supplemental daily doses of vitamins and minerals.

In today's world, it's difficult to get all the nutrients your body requires from diet alone. The soil contains fewer minerals today than it did a century ago, which means that foods grown in that soil are lacking in those minerals. Your body's need for nutrients is on the rise as well because of constant exposure to chemical toxins, pollutants, and high levels of stress. And no matter how hard you try, there are bound to be some days when you can't eat enough good foods and you eat a few too many bad ones instead.

Not everyone requires the same vitamin and mineral supplementation program. Below, you'll find my basic program, which is a good starting point for any adult who wants some extra protection against disease and premature aging. Many multivitamins will give you the dosages listed below. Look for one that dissolves readily (see page 43 for a simple test using vinegar that will show you how easily your supplements dissolve), is small enough to swallow easily, uses natural vitamins rather than synthetic versions, and doesn't use starch or colorings. If you can find one made with whole food concentrates rather than isolated vitamins, you'll be getting a broader spectrum of nutrients.

Look for a high-potency multiple vitamin to take at least twice a day that gives you the following:

Vitamins

B_1 (thiamine)	25–50 mg
B_2 (niacin)	25–100 mg
B_3 (riboflavin)	25–100 mg
B_4 (pantothenic acid)	25–100 mg
B_5 (pyridoxine)	50–100 mg
B_{12}	500–1,000 mcg
Biotin	100–300 mcg
Beta-carotene or carotenoids	10,000–15,000 IU
Choline	25–100 mg
Folic acid	200–400 mcg
Inositol	100–300 mg
Vitamin C	1,000–3,000 mg
Vitamin D	100–500 IU
Vitamin E	at least 400 IU total per day

Minerals

Boron	1–5 mg
Calcium (citrate, lactate, or gluconate)	100–500 mg (women should take a total of 600–1,200 mg daily)
Chromium (picolinate)	200–400 mcg
Copper	1–5 mg
Magnesium (citrate or gluconate)	100–500 mg (women should take a total of 300–600 mg daily)
Manganese (citrate or chelate)	10 mg
Selenium	25–50 mcg
Vanadium (vanadyl sulfate)	25–200 mcg
Zinc	10–15 mg

Since vitamin C, vitamin E, calcium, and magnesium tend to make a multivitamin larger, you can take a multivitamin with smaller amounts of those vitamins and then take the others separately. A calcium/magnesium combination taken at bedtime will help you relax and prevent leg cramps.

GLOSSARY

absorption The process by which nutrients are passed into the bloodstream through the walls of the intestines.

acetic acid The acidic component of vinegar, made from alcohol during the second fermentation to vinegar; used as a synthetic flavoring agent; one of the first food additives (vinegar is approximately 4 to 6 percent acetic acid); found naturally in cheese, coffee, grapes, peaches, raspberries, and strawberries.

acetobacter The aerobic bacteria that transform alcohol to acetic acid during the making of vinegar.

acid A substance with a pH below 7 on a scale of 1 to 14.

aerobic Requiring oxygen.

alkaline A substance with a pH above 7 on a scale of 1 to 14; alkaline substances neutralize acids.

amino acids The organic compounds from which proteins are constructed; twenty-two amino acids have been identified as necessary to the human body; nine are known as essential—histidine, isoleucine, leucine, lysine, total S-containing amino acids, total aromatic amino acids, threonine, tryptophan, and valine—and must be obtained from food.

antioxidant A substance that can protect another substance from oxidation; thought to protect against diseases, including cancer and heart disease; aids in function of immune system; added to foods to keep oxygen from changing the food's color.

arthritis Pain, erosion, or inflammation of joints.

assimilation The process whereby nutrients are used by the body and changed into living tissue.

asthma A condition of the lungs characterized by a decrease in the diameter of some air passages; a spasm of the bronchial tubes or swelling of their mucous membranes.

bacteria A group of single-celled microorganisms, some of which cause disease.

beta-carotene A plant pigment that can be converted into two forms of vitamin A; helps to prevent cancer and improves vision.

bicarbonate An alkaline substance released from the pancreas in response to acidic foods such as vinegar.

bile A substance made by the liver and stored in the gallbladder; needed for the digestion and assimilation of fats from the diet.

bioflavonoids A group of compounds needed to maintain healthy blood vessel walls; found chiefly as coloring matter in flowers and fruits, particularly yellow ones; known as vitamin P complex.

biotin A colorless, crystalline B complex vitamin; essential for the activity of many enzyme systems; helps produce fatty acids; found in large quantities in liver, egg yolk, milk, and yeast.

calciferol A colorless, odorless crystalline material, insoluble in water; soluble in fats; a synthetic form of vitamin D made by irradiating ergosterol with ultraviolet light.

calcium citrate An easily assimilated form of calcium, derived from eggshells; a homemade calcium citrate supplement can be made with vinegar and eggshells.

carcinogen A cancer-causing substance.

cardiovascular Relating to the heart and blood vessels.

carotene Any one of 600 orange-yellow pigments occuring in many plants, including beta-carotene; also called *carotenoids;* some are capable of being converted into vitamin A in the body.

chelation A process by which mineral substances are changed into an easily digestible form.

cholesterol A white, crystalline substance, made up of various fats; naturally produced in vertebrate animals and humans; important as a precursor to steroid hormones and as a constituent of cell membranes.

chronic Of long duration, continuing, constant.

coenzyme A substance that combines with other substances to form a complete enzyme; nonprotein and usually a B vitamin.

complex carbohydrate Fibrous molecules of starch or sugar that slowly release sugar into the bloodstream.

diuretic Tending to increase the flow of urine from the body.

enteric coated A tablet coated so that it dissolves in the intestine, not in the acid environment of the stomach.

enzyme A protein substance found in living cells that brings about chemical changes; necessary for digestion of food; compounds with names ending in -*ase*.

fermentation The process by which bacteria or yeasts transform foods, endowing them with unique nutritional properties.

fiber The nondigestible part of plant foods; can be soluble (can be dissolved in water) or unsoluble (cannot be dissolved in water).

free radicals Highly reactive chemical fragments that can beneficially act as chemical messengers, but that in excess produce an irritation of artery walls and start the arteriosclerotic process if antioxidants are not present.

gallbladder A sac under the liver where bile is stored and concentrated.

gallstones Round or oval, smooth or faceted lumps of solid matter found in the gallbladder. Sometimes these stones can become lodged in the bile ducts, causing intense pain in the upper right side of the abdomen or between the shoulder blades.

glucose Blood sugar; a product of the body's assimilation of carbohydrates and a major source of energy.

HDL High-density lipoprotein; HDL is sometimes called "good" cholesterol because it is the body's major carrier of cholesterol to the liver for excretion in the bile.

heart attack Also called myocardial infarction; caused by lack of oxygen to the heart muscle through the vessels that bring oxygen-rich blood to its walls; may be due to buildup of fatty tissues in the coronary arteries, or to spasm of coronary artery walls.

hormone A substance formed in endocrine organs and transported by body fluids to activate other specifically receptive organs, cells, or tissues.

hydrochloric acid An acid secreted in the stomach; a main part of gastric juice.

immune Protected against disease.

inflammation Heat, swelling, redness, and pain created when the body mounts an immune response; healthy in moderation, but often can spiral out of control; if it is not controlled, can cause tissue damage.

insulin A hormone, secreted by the pancreas, that helps regulate the metabolism of sugar in the body.

interferon Any of a group of proteins produced by cells in response to infection by a virus; prevents viral replication and can induce resistance to viral antigens.

IU International Units.

kidney stones Small stones, usually composed of calcium, which can begin to move toward the bladder, causing severe pain and even bleeding into the urine.

LDL Low-density lipoprotein; sometimes referred to as "bad" cholesterol, LDLs easily become oxidized and carry cholesterol through the bloodstream; studies show high levels can increase risk of coronary artery disease (CAD).

metabolism The processes of physical and chemical change whereby food is synthesised into living matter until it is broken

down into simpler substances or waste matter; energy is produced
by these processes.

mother of vinegar The living "mat" of *acetobacter* that forms on
fermenting vinegar, transforming alcohol to acetic acid.

naturopath One who heals with the use of herbs and other
methods to stimulate the body's innate defenses without
using drugs.

omega-3 oils Found in deepwater fish and flaxseeds; have anti-
inflammatory, heart-protective, and anticancer effects.

organic Any food or supplement made with animal or vegetable
fertilizers, or produced without synthetic fertilizers or pesticides and
free from chemical injections or additives.

oxidation The way in which certain types of altered oxygen molecules cause biochemical reactions; examples are browning of apples
and rancidity in oil.

PABA Para-aminobenzoic acid; a member of the vitamin B complex.

palmitate Water-solubilized vitamin A.

pectin A fiberlike substance found in apples and other fruits.

pH Stands for *potential hydrogens;* indicates the acidity or alkalinity
of a liquid.

phytochemical Any chemical found naturally in plants that is
neither vitamin nor mineral.

phytoestrogen Phytochemicals that occupy estrogen receptors
and may help protect the body from the negative effects of excess
estrogen.

probiotic "Friendly" bacteria that perform important health-
promoting functions in the human body, such as making vitamins,
fostering good digestion, and keeping yeasts and "unfriendly"
bacteria from overgrowing.

protein A complex substance containing nitrogen, which is essential to plant and animal cells; ingested proteins are changed to
amino acids in the body.

provitamin A vitamin precursor; a chemical substance necessary to produce a vitamin.

riboflavin Vitamin B_2; part of the B vitamin complex; yellow, crystal-like coenzyme involved in the breakdown of proteins, fats, and carbohydrates; must be obtained from food.

rose hip A rich source of vitamin C; the nodule underneath the bud of a rose, called a hip, in which the plant produces vitamin C.

rutin A substance often extracted from buckwheat; part of the vitamin C complex.

simple carbohydrate Simple sugar molecules, such as glucose, which are rapidly absorbed by the bloodstream.

tocopherols The group of compounds (alpha, beta, delta, epsilon, eta, gamma, and zeta) that make vitamin E; obtained through vacuum distillation of edible vegetable oils.

toxicity The quality or condition of being poisonous, harmful, or destructive.

toxin A poison produced in living organisms or found in nonliving substances.

virus Any of a large group of minute organisms that can only reproduce in the cells of plants and animals.

vitamin Any of about fifteen natural compounds essential in small amounts as catalysts for processes in the body; most cannot be made by the body and must come from the diet.

yeast Single-celled fungus that can cause infections in the body.

SOURCES AND RECOMMENDED READING

Bragg, P. C., and P. Bragg. *Apple Cider Vinegar Miracle Health System.* Santa Barbara, Calif. Health Science, 1999.

Brighenti, F. et al., "Effect of Neutralized and Native Vinegar on Blood Glucose and Acetate Responses to a Mixed Meal in Healthy Subjects." *European Journal of Clinical Nutrition* 49, no. 4 (April 1995) 242–47.

Creber, A. *Vinegars.* Australia: Angus & Robertson, 1990.

Eberhardt, M. V., C. Y. Lee, and R. H. Liu, "Antioxidant Activity of Fresh Apples," *Nature* 405, no. 6789 (June 22, 2000): 903–4.

Frisch, L. E., F. H. Milner, and D. G. Ferris. "Naked-Eye Inspection of the Cervix after Acetic Acid Application May Improve the Predictive Value of Negative Cytologic Screening." *Journal of Family Practice* 39, no. 5 (November 1994): 457–60.

Jarvis, D. C. *Folk Medicine: A Vermont Doctor's Guide to Good Health.* New York: Holt, Rhinehart and Winston, 1958.

Orey, C. *The Healing Powers of Vinegar.* New York: Kensington Books, 2000.

Ravnskov, U. *The Cholesterol Myths.* Washington, D.C.: New Trends Publishing, 2000.

Schaafsma, A., P. J. deVries, and W. H. Saris. "Delay of Natural Bone Loss by Higher Intakes of Specific Minerals and Vitamins." *Critical Review of Food Science Nutrition* 41, no. 4 (May 2001): 225–49.

Thacker, E. *The Vinegar Book.* Canton, Ohio: Tresco Publishers, 1995.

Quillin, P. *Honey, Garlic, and Vinegar: Home Remedies and Recipes.* North Canton, Ohio: The Leader Co., Inc., 1996.

Watson, B. *Cider: Hard and Sweet.* Woodstock, Vt.: The Countryman Press, 1999.

INDEX